Tallahassee Writers Association

SEVEN HILLS REVIEW
2019

Volume 24

The Seven Hills Review and Penumbra Poetry Contest is an annual project of the Tallahassee Writers Association. All screening, judging, manuscript preparation, artwork, etc., are volunteer efforts of the Tallahassee Writers Association and our contributors.

Current planned categories and descriptions for the Summer of 2019 are at the back of this volume. For the latest information on entering and entry criteria, be sure to check for updates at **www.twaonline.org**.

ISBN-13: 978 10923 95403
Manuscript Layout: Rhiannon Green
Managing Editor: Bruce Ballister
Cover Photo: Bruce Ballister, 2017

Contents

Penumbra Poetry and Haiku Competition

The Judging Process

Our 2018 judges were selected for their particular expertise, experience, and standing in their specific category. Our readers are volunteer members of the Tallahassee Writers Association who donated countless hours reading through the (often numerous) submissions in their categories. Creative Non-Fiction and Short Story each received fifteen entries. Adult Novel Excerpts received eighteen, while Young Adult Novel received sixteen. Our Poetry readers read through forty-two entries, and the Haiku readers had to choose the best of fifty-two entries. All judging was blind; any entries with names attached to the primary submission were disqualified. We have to ensure that no preference is shown to submitters known to our judges. Each reader gave a yes, maybe, or no verdict on each submission. The results were made available to finalist judges through the Submittable software platform.

Our finalist judges had the freedom to follow the recommendations of the pre-readers or to dig into the digital pile of files, mining for nuggets. In many of the categories, the judges agreed with our readers, but in a few, the search for the best required the additional effort. We think you'll agree that some real gems have been found. Our winning writers span the continent with contestants from California to Georgia and even Ontario. This year we again had the result of multiple winners in more than one category. Congratulations to all our winners.

For our readers, we hope you'll enjoy the 24th Volume of the series, the *2019 Seven Hills Review* and hope you will follow up on the full versions of excerpted submissions. I welcome you to peruse the back of the book for the brief introductions to our winners and judges. Thank you all.

Bruce Ballister, Managing Editor
The Seven Hills Review
Tallahassee Writers Association

THE SEVEN HILLS LITERARY COMPETITION

Adult Novel Excerpt
Final Judge—Darryl Bollinger
Waynesville, North Carolina

First Place—Summer of '85
Richard Fellinger—Camp Hill, Pennsylvania

I hear about the shooting while driving home from the office. I'm tuned to a country station, and after a ditty by a guy singing lovingly about his truck, the DJ comes on and promises traffic and weather, but first she has breaking news. In her bumpkin voice, she says, "News out of Philly isn't good, not at all. It seems there's been a shooting in Center City, at least a dozen possible victims. It's being described as an active shooter scene at a hoagie shop. We'll have more as we get more information, but now, the ..."

I get home and click on CNN, toss my jacket on a chair in the corner. Wolf Blitzer is doing a voice-over as a helicopter camera pans an entire city block at dusk, red police lights swirling. It's hard to see much in detail, except police cars parked at odd angles, the heads and shoulders of cops and ambulance workers rushing around. The news bar at the bottom of the screen reads, "BREAKING: A DOZEN REPORTED KILLED IN PHILLY MASS SHOOTING."

As I settle into the couch, with a mushy pillow propped behind my back, our three-legged terrier hops up on my lap and licks at my hands. His name is Wimpy, born without a left front leg, but that doesn't stop him from bouncing up on the furniture. We found him as a puppy three years ago at a local rescue, and though Stacey had her heart set on a chocolate lab, I saw the three-legged pup and talked her into adopting him. I realize he wants his dinner right now, but he'll have to wait. I want to hear what Wolf has to say.

Details are still sketchy, Wolf says, but the scene is a hoagie shop called Billy G's. My wife and I have been there before, only once, during a weekend getaway to the art museum a few years back. The place is famous for its Italian pork, and while the Center City shop is the flagship, chains have popped up across the region, from Atlantic City to Harrisburg. The shooting started at the dinner hour.

It's unclear who the shooter is, Wolf says, or whether he's still alive or on the scene. An unarmed Middle Eastern man was seen running from the block immediately after the shooting, but his connection to the shooting, if any, is unknown. An eyewitness from a bakery across the street saw one masked shooter carrying an assault-style rifle inside the hoagie shop, but police have not yet confirmed it.

We live in Harrisburg, where I'm the editorial page editor for the local newspaper, *The Telegraph*. We're two hours west of Philly, close enough that we might expect some local connections to the story, maybe even a local victim. I log onto my phone and check our site, which links to a one-sentence news flash from the Associated Press. It says nothing I don't already know but promises updates soon.

I text our editor-in-chief, Norm Baker, asking, "Need anything from me?" A few minutes later I get a reply: "Not now. Just sent two reporters to Philly. Start thinking about follow-up editorials."

As dusk turns to dark, CNN is still showing the street scene from above, and even less is discernible now, mostly just whirling red lights. Wolf hands the coverage to

Erin Burnett, who then hands off to Anderson Cooper. Anderson interviews a former FBI guy, a retired police commissioner, and the author of a book on mass shootings. They discuss police tactics, ruminate on whether the shooter is still at large or might be holding hostages, and speculate about the possibility of terrorism, but nobody really knows anything. Then Anderson interrupts the author, urgency in his voice, and says there's word the shooter is down, apparently killed himself in the back kitchen of Billy G's. Police believe there's only one shooter, but they still want to question the Middle Eastern guy. The news bar changes to, "BREAKING: PHILLY MASS SHOOTER FOUND DEAD IN APPARENT SUICIDE."

Then comes news of a reaction from the President. He tweets, "Sending thoughts and prayers to the victims and families in the Philly shooting. Law enforcement is on the scene, doing a FANTASTIC job!"

There was a time when I would have been on the way to that bloody scene. Back when I was younger, a cops reporter. That was before I was promoted to assistant city editor, then city editor, then editorial page editor, a nine-to-five job that I secured five years ago. Now I'm stuck in the first grips of middle age, married with no kids, sitting only with our dog in our quiet twin home in uptown Harrisburg, watching the scene unfold from my tan Crate & Barrel couch, my favorite soft pillow cushioning my back, my only duty to think about follow-up editorials. And feed the dog.

So finally, I feed the dog, let him out to pee. Meanwhile, I warm up a leftover plate of lasagna.

Stacey comes home, keys dangling in her hand, and sees that I'm tuned to the coverage, plate in my lap. Wimpy hobbles across the room and paws at her knees, tail wagging giddily. "Can you believe this?" Stacey says. She's a campaign pro, working this year for a Republican attorney general candidate, so she often comes home late. She eases into the couch beside me, still wearing her jacket, still holding her keys. We gawk at the screen together for a moment, shake our heads in disbelief.

"It happened at Billy G's," I say. "Do you remember going there for lunch?"

"Of course," she says, and there's wistfulness in her voice, as if it reminds her of a different, better time.

I sleep fitfully, wake up early the next morning, make coffee and open my laptop at the kitchen counter. By now, we have details—*The Telegraph*'s Web site has a full story from the two reporters Norm sent to Philly. Eleven people dead, plus the shooter. Eight more hospitalized, and three are critical. No cops injured. All nineteen victims were patrons or employees of Billy G's, but police are still notifying victims' families and have not yet released any names.

The shooter is identified as Bernard Lazzarro, twenty-six years old, who was recently fired from his job as a cook at Billy G's. No word yet on why he was fired. He lived with his mother in Southwest Philly. He toted one AR-15 semi-automatic rifle and a 9-mm semi-automatic pistol. No word yet on how he obtained the guns.

I lug my thermal mug of coffee into the newspaper office, mulling another editorial on gun control. I also have to give careful consideration to when to run it. File it for the next day's paper, or wait a day or two? There's good reason to wait, especially in conservative Central Pennsylvania, where I'm a bit of an outlier. In a region full of farmers, hunters, and evangelicals, my politics are center-left. My readers often call me a dyed-in-the-wool liberal, and the worst of them call me a socialist. So I don't want to be accused of politicizing another gun tragedy before the tears are dry. Besides, I need job security—I'm at that age where it's prudent to plan for retirement, so I recently upped my 401K contribution to ten percent of my salary. Whenever possible, I'm conflict avoidant, and I'm okay with that. I've seen enough of the world, and I know my place.

So I'm inclined to wait.

Late morning, Norm comes by my desk. He's a spindly guy with mussy gray-blonde hair and John Lennon glasses—looks more like a history professor than a newspaper guy. But in fact he's a newspaper lifer who's well-liked in the newsroom, even though he's often steamrolled by the number-crunching publisher. Yet during years of declining ad revenues and staff cutbacks, Norm has held the newsroom together pretty well.

"How's your thing, Dan?" he asks. He's referring to a suspicious lesion on my back, which my doctor removed a few days ago.

"Good—it was benign," I say.

"Glad to hear it," he says. "I have to go in next week for a colonoscopy. Not looking forward to it."

"I understand," I say.

"So what are you thinking for editorials?"

"Something respectful for tomorrow," I say. "Something about the need for the community to come together. The next day, another call for gun control. I want to wait a day on that so we're not accused of pushing an agenda before the smoke even clears."

"Sounds good," he says agreeably. He's an agreeable guy.

After he leaves, I play a few games of computer solitaire. I lose most of them.

Eventually, I open a new Word document and start drafting the next day's editorial, checking the wire every now and then for updates about the shooting. More details trickle in as the day crawls along. Lazzarro's car, an old Chevy Malibu, is found in a parking garage down the street from Billy G's with more guns in the trunk. His Facebook photo circulates on the wires. He's small-shouldered and baby-faced, and in the photo he's wearing a gray T-shirt and holding a handgun across his chest. He's a white guy, and on his Facebook profile, under political views, he lists "Confederate." His mother is refusing to talk to reporters, but investigators say she's cooperating with them. Police also say the Middle Eastern guy seen running from the scene had no connection to the shooting.

Almost half the victims are identified, but none are from the Harrisburg area. They're from the city or its inner suburbs such as Cherry Hill and Conshohocken. At Thomas Jefferson University Hospital, one critical victim is upgraded to stable.

In the newsroom, Norm instructs our two reporters in Philly to file one more story with all the latest details and then drive back to Harrisburg. We'll run Associated Press follow-ups after that.

My editorial for the next day begins with the obvious: *Once again, a community has been ravaged by gun violence, this one fairly close to home.* It segues into a passage about remembering the victims, then one about the need for the community to come together to heal. It finishes with a plea to government officials at all levels to work together to end gun violence, but it's vague enough that it shouldn't offend anyone. All in all, I must admit, it doesn't say much.

At the afternoon editor's meeting, when I lay out my editorial plans for the next couple of days, there are yes nods all around the table. Even Marcia Barber keeps her trap shut. As managing editor, number-two at the paper behind Norm, Marcia is our most outspoken Second Amendment Sister. She's a stout woman with stringy hair who lives south of town on a hillside in York County, and her husband is an avid hunter and Civil War reenactor. Maybe I've silenced her today by proposing to wait a day until pushing the gun-control button, or maybe, as a reenactor's wife, she's embarrassed by the revelation that there are murderous kooks out there still claiming an allegiance to confederate politics.

Late afternoon, more details. Lazzarro, who had no criminal record, bought all of his guns legally. He was fired from Billy G's a week ago for repeatedly making insensitive racial remarks on the job and had been warned previously. He wore a long black jacket as he mowed down his victims, and likely concealed the AR-15 under the jacket as he marched from the parking garage to the hoagie shop. He donned a black ski mask outside the door. His neighbors describe him as a quiet guy who rarely ventured outside, except to shovel in snowstorms or take out the trash.

I file my editorial and head home to feed the dog.

I'm back on the couch, Wimpy in my lap, sipping a scotch, when Stacey comes home. Unlike last night, when we were both stunned by the initial news of a mass shooting two hours away, she's in a scrappy mood.

"So I suppose you'll be running another gun control editorial tomorrow," she says, hanging her jacket on the coat rack in the corner. "No reason to wait for the blood to dry, right?"

"Actually, we're going to let it dry." I say, stroking the dog's back. "For a day, at least."

"Wow, and you call that editorial restraint?"

I like this side of her, always have. My wife is no Second Amendment Sister, but she's a loyal and feisty Republican. I'm a lifelong Democrat—or Dumbocrat, as she likes to call me—and when we first met ten years ago, we found ourselves bantering like this all the time. So our relationship immediately had a James Carville-Mary Matalin quality to it, or at least the flirtier version, Joe Scarborough-Mika Brzezinski. Stacey's five years younger than me, but she's as smart as she looks with her tortoiseshell glasses, bob-styled brown hair and cuddle-with-me face. Unfortunately, we don't jest as much as we used to. Or cuddle. Time has straddled our marriage with all the usual little problems.

"Plus," I say in my best deadpan voice, "another gun control editorial means less work for me. All I have to do is cut and paste the one from the last shooting, and call it a day. I don't think anyone will even notice."

"Ha, ha," she says mockingly. She plops onto the opposite end of the couch and puts her feet up on our Origami coffee table. After a minute, she pulls out her phone and fingers it.

On CNN, Anderson Cooper is about to cut to commercial, but first he asks his viewers to watch a video collage of the names and photos of the victims. I sip my scotch, sorta paying attention as names and faces fade on and off the screen against a soundtrack of soft piano music.

The last name and face stun me.

Cara Cassaday.

Curly reddish hair, green eyes, dimpled cheeks, light freckles. There are age lines in her skin, but she's still beautiful.

"My God!" I lunge off the couch, spilling scotch on my pants, sending the dog tumbling to the floor.

"What is it?" Stacey asks.

"I dated her," I confess, pointing at the screen. I'm too jolted, too unnerved to say anything but the simple truth. "One summer, years ago."

Cara's face fades to black, then a Hyundai ad.

Second Place—*Collision Orbit*
Rebekah Davis—Bishop, California

The scarred, battered hull of an old star freighter shuddered and clawed its way back into normal space. Its occupants held on for dear life against the vibration in the hull and the surges in the ships gravity field. In the darkened passageways of the crew berthing area, a giant of a man in simple clothes sat at a steel table looking at a star chart on his tablet. The ship's chronometer on the bulkhead behind the man indicated that it was the middle of third watch, ship's time, and most of the crew were asleep. The few that were awake were either on watch in the bridge compartment or manning the computer consoles in engineering.

Jim Donovan looked away from his tablet and stared intently at an older man lying in the bunk to his left. The old man's face was a kaleidoscope of bruises, knots, and lacerations. Underneath all the technicolor, the skin had the ghastly pallor of coming death. Craig Wellborn was a dying man. Too much damage had occurred internally and much too quickly for Craig to recover. There was no medical help on the ship beyond a first aid kit and the skills of the crew. Those skills proved woefully inadequate to the task of saving Craig's life.

Craig awakened and turned his head toward Jim. "Remember, Jim, you made me a promise. I will hold you to it. Please take care of this for me. I can't."

Jim reached for Craig's hand and held it as he looked steadily into the eyes of his dying friend. "Don't you fret, Craig, we are getting off this tub tonight. We are almost close enough to reach the mining outpost with the lifeboat. All the supplies have been stored carefully away and the sensors have been fudged up to look as if the boat is still in its nacelle even after we've left."

"No," replied Craig, "you and I both know I am never getting out of this bunk. Please, just do what I asked. That will be enough. I know you are man enough to see this through. Watch out for Barton. He's mean, sneaky, and smart. When he finds out you own half the place, he will kill you soon as look at ya."

With that, Craig turned his face back to the bulkhead and faded off to sleep. Somewhere in the darkness, his breathing slowed and finally stopped. There was a quiet rattle and then complete silence.

Jim pulled the blanket up over Craig's face, checked his tablet once more, slowly stood up and started out of the bunk room. Jim had to stoop going through the door as his six-foot two-inch frame was a bit too tall for the opening. Barely wide enough for his shoulders, he could walk through, but habit caused him to turn a bit sideways in the opening. When he came to the next portal, he tapped softly on the bulkhead and two more spacers answered the knock.

"Wellborn is dead, is everything ready?"

Joshua Kelly replied, "yep. We have enough freeze-dried rations and water to last us for a month if necessary. The boat is loaded and ready to shove off when you are. The Second mate caught us with the last of the food and he decided it was better to go for a walk outside the hull. I am thinking he will not be missed before the ship makes landfall. Are you still going through with your plans? You don't have to. All we need do is get in the life boat and take off."

"Nope, said Jim. You and Garcia be in the boat and ready to travel when I get there. This is something that's needed doing since I came aboard. I am going to enjoy this right enough."

Jim turned and walked up the passage toward the bridge. The rest of the command team was locked in the brig, victims of the drugged liquor they seized from Craig's duffle bag. The man Jim wanted to see was the Captain, and he wanted to see him rather badly. The Captain was a big mean sonofabitch that fought hand to hand most of the time and he fought dirty. The Captain loved to bully the spacers around and simply, sadistically, enjoyed beating the hell out of the weaker ones.

Jim Donovan reflected on his life as he walked closer to the final confrontation with Captain Vargas. Donovan was a hired soldier of fortune. A mercenary for hire for anyone with the funds and a battle to fight. A bit over a year ago, having finished a contract with Sergio De la Vega on New Spain, Jim had spent his last night on the planet at a bar near the space port.

As he always hated to drink alone, he found a new friend in an older man. Craig Wellborn was open, honest, educated, and ebullient. Although the two men were from far distant backgrounds, it was an instant bond and a strong friendship began. Craig and Jim talked and drank and wandered from one spaceport dive to another. At the very last one, something was added to their drinks besides alcohol and the two men woke up two days later with splitting headaches aboard the star freighter Carlita and a hell of a long way from New Spain.

Just after waking in the brig, Captain Vargas came in and introduced his self by cold cocking Craig and then having the first mate throw a bucket of water on the old man. Jim could not retaliate because the second mate and one of the crewmen held blasters on him.

Vargas told them they were conscripts and needed to keep their mouths shut and do the work assigned them without complaint or the repercussions would be dire, indeed. Jim asked when they would be released and where and Vargas snarled out "when you are dead."

Jim's response was to snarl back and the crewman butt-stroked him with the blaster rifle stock. When Jim got back on his feet, the Captain glared at him and promised more of the same for non-compliance. "Do your jobs and do them well and you will be rewarded with food. Fail in any manner and out the airlock you go."

Jim decided it best to bide his time and wait for better odds. Besides, it was a long empty walk back to New Spain and no way to survive the vacuum except in the ship. Having served time in many space battles, Jim was a consummate Able Spacer and quite capable of performing almost any task aboard the freighter, from manning the helm to maintaining the engines and engineering department.

With complete disregard for his skills, the first mate had Jim cleaning and swabbing the ship from stem to stern. Craig ended up in the galley washing dishes and peeling spuds. It was inevitable that the two of them shared a berthing area and soon two others joined their little coffee klatch in the evenings when off duty. Joshua Kelly and Diego Garcia rounded out the foursome. Sometimes playing cards, sometimes they just talked. Gradually, they got to know each other and their backgrounds.

Craig Wellborn was a cattleman on New Spain. According to his story, he owned a nice ranch in a little river valley west of Toledo in one of the many under-developed areas on the planet. The grass was tall and rich and easily supported his small herd of 1,000 cattle. There was water enough as a small river ran out of the mountains down through the valley. Pure, clear melt water from winter snows in the mountains and several springs along the river kept the grass green and the livestock watered.

The downside was that Craig had borrowed money from an investor named Barton in a nearby town to buy the brood stock. Having made the interest payments for several years to keep the note active, Craig had finally sold enough cattle to pay off the note. He made a drive to the stockyards in Toledo near the spaceport, sold the herd, paid off his men and supposedly met Barton and paid off the mortgage. Craig had the signed note with him and it showed the balance paid in full.

He had been out celebrating the event when he ran into Jim and then ended up in the clutches of Captain Vargas.

Jim had drifted from one battle to another since he was eighteen years old. In between battles, he worked the bars and pleasures palaces of the frontier towns on the new worlds. By the time he met Craig, he had fought in dozens of battles, from Vega to Betelgeuse, all throughout the Orion cluster. He never talked about his childhood or anything else that happened to him before he signed up for the military service.

Diego Garcia and Joshua Kelly were miners and ranch hands. New Spain was a mineralogical treasure house and its wealth had barely begun to be explored let alone exploited. They could always find work in the mines, but they had tired of working for the other guy and wanted to prospect a bit on their own. Having saved up their money, they were having one last fling in civilization before heading out to the minefields to stake a claim. In fact, Diego was a degreed mining engineer and had some good ideas about where he and Joshua could find a spot and build a working mine.

All of this went through Jim's head as he walked carefully toward the Captain's cabin just off the bridge. When he knocked on the door, Vargas growled, "enter". Surprised that he was awake at this hour, Jim open the door and stepped into the room. The Captain was sitting at his desk with an open bottle of bourbon, and had obviously been sampling the liquor, but as his capacity was huge, he was hardly incapacitated. He shoved his chair back from desk and stood up deliberately facing Jim.

"So," said Vargas, "you have come for your final beating, eh? Well, Senor, I, Emilio Vargas will be most honored to give it to you. After I beat you bloody, I will drag what's left of your carcass to the airlock and blow you out into the vacuum. It is cold out there, no?"

Barrell-chested, with arms like tree trunks, Vargas stupidly charged into Jim, thinking he would bulldoze him into the steel bulkhead and stun him right off the bat. Jim, however, had other ideas about the outcome. Veteran of dozens of battles, experienced with weaponry ranging from gunpowder rifles to blasters to tactical nukes, Jim had fought hand-to-hand both barehanded and with an assortment of hand weapons, this fight he would win without a doubt.

Vargas was powerful, and someone to be wary of, but he did not know what he was up against in Jim. Vargas was a bully and used bully tactics. Jim fought scientifically, coolly, and methodically, reducing his opponent to defeat. Vargas never laid a hand on Jim. Jim sidestepped Vargas' charge by pivoting on one foot, bringing the other around and shoving Vargas into the very bulkhead intended for him. Vargas fetched up against the steel with a wet squish as his nose broke and blood splattered.

As he bounced off the wall, Jim caught him by the collar, spun him around and sank his right into the man's solar plexus. Vargas doubled over only to be met with Jim's left in a powerful upper cut that laid the older man out sprawling on the deck. Vargas groaned one time, tried to force himself back to his feet and then fell back unconscious.

Jim spotted the cash box on the desk, opened it and carefully counted out the wages for him and his friends for the year they had been on board. Stuffing the credits in is pants pocket, he took his leave of the Captain and hurried to the lifeboat deck.

With his two friends aboard, Jim powered up the ship's drive and initiated the launch sequence in the computer. The nacelle hatch split open and a small hydraulic ram shoved the small craft out into space. Once free of the freighter, Jim pulled up the course computer and plugged in the proper course for the New Toledo spaceport. He had in mind a small field at a remote mining outpost outside of town where he could ditch the lifeboat.

As small as the boat was, he could make landfall without showing up on the control radar at the spaceport, but he would have to land several kilometers away from town. It couldn't be helped, he and the others would just have to walk into town. Perhaps there, with the credits he and the others had earned, they could acquire some transport.

Third Place—*Pay Attention*
Francis Hicks—San Antonio, Texas

A guy pulled into the toll plaza in an old rusty Rambler with the windows rolled down. He stopped in front of me and leaned across the front seat. "Where you headed?"

I squatted next to the passenger window. The sides of the driver's head were shaved boot-camp short. He wore a boonie hat with the chin strap hanging down. My long hair reflected in the lenses of his mirrored sunglasses.

The tension in his jaw creeped me out. I assumed he was just back from Nam. The National Guard had recently shot those four kids in Ohio, so anything even remotely military made me nervous.

I tried to swallow, but my throat was too dry. "West. To Milwaukee, eventually."

"Well, I'm goin' quite a ways in that direction and would be happy ta help you out, but I had a boy in the car a while back that pulled a knife and cut me pretty bad. I'll give you a ride, but you hafta wear handcuffs while you're in the car. Whaddya think?"

My eyes played over the four lanes that lead to the toll booths. Not another car in sight. No place to get out of the sun. My heart sank at the thought of being stuck here another four hours. I stood and backed away from the car. "I'll wait it out."

"Huh. Didn't figure you for such a pussy." The man settled back into the driver's seat. Tires squealed as he peeled off, leaving a cloud of exhaust smoke.

I slumped down on my pack again, still pissed that my so-called friend Jim bailed on me and took off with that girl. Jesus! "C'mon, Nate," he'd said back in Milwaukee. "I know people. I'll make sure we get back safe."

Lying asshole. All he wanted was the $50.00 he knew I had. But, I desperately wanted to be liked so, even knowing his crappy motives, I had agreed to go. Now I was on my own dealing with crazy people like the handcuff guy. So much for making friends. Why can't everybody be like me? If I ran the world everyone would get along.

I was hungry, hot, smelly, exhausted from nights half-awake watching my backpack, worrying over my last three dollars, afraid of what might happen the next time I got into a car. I'd been stuck at this New York Thruway toll plaza all morning, and it was driving me crazy. Hitchhiking had seemed so exciting when Jim suggested it, but after two weeks of bored misery, interrupted by an adrenaline rush every time a car slowed down, followed by anxiety at what might happen if I got in, hitchhiking sucked. I had no relief from sun, rain, or fear. I just wanted to get back home, even though home was not a happy place.

It wasn't the destination I longed for, but an end to the journey. My Catholic mother, with her pointed verbal warnings and intermittent silent stares, regularly reminded me of the dangers of hell. It wore on me because the priests reinforced this belief. I mostly believed her and them. I feared God and feared her.

Dad was an "America, love it or leave it" type, always bragging about my brother's two tours in Vietnam. Pete made it home safe, even said he liked it over there. But I hated the war, mostly because I was scared of getting my ass shot off. They hadn't drafted me yet, and I told dad I wasn't going to go if they did. He called me a coward. Maybe I was, but at least I would have a better chance at a long life.

Fatigue weighed on my eyelids until I drifted off. A blaring horn shot me awake. Three guys in a convertible flew past. The driver yelled, "Get a job, you fucking hippie."

I threw my hands up and extended my middle fingers, partly from anger, but mostly from surprise. Brake lights lit up. The car skidded to a stop and sat idling.

The driver looked in the mirror.

Oh shit. I stood and picked up my backpack, eyes locked on the guys in the convertible. An ass whipping seemed likely. I looked around the plaza for a place to disappear, but it was just a wide spot in the road before the toll booth.

The car backed up. It was a shiny, new Cutlass 442. The driver wore sunglasses and was about my age, maybe a little older.

"Hey," he said. "Where you headed?"

I stared at him, trying to figure out how to answer. He didn't *look* hostile. He smiled with white, straight teeth. The guy next to him was tuning the radio. The rider in the back seat had his head down like he was asleep. All I could see of him was a mass of matted, black curly hair. He seemed different from the other two, out of it, like he was in a different time zone. Just like in junior high, it was three against me.

"West," I said.

"Well, jump on in. We've got room." He raised his eyebrows and pursed his lips, then said, "We're going all the way to Cleveland."

Sweat dripped into my eyes and my head itched. I desperately wanted a ride, but the guys in front were slightly older versions of the kids that used beat me up.

"Cleveland? That's quite a ways, but you guys just called me a fucking hippie." I pushed my hair out of my face. "I mean, I am a hippie, proud of it. But you don't seem to dig it."

The driver looked at me sideways. "Look, let's start over. This is Sean." He pointed to the passenger, "and I'm Brian. We were just messing with you. What do you say? Jump on in."

I wanted to believe him. At least he hadn't asked me to wear handcuffs. Still, something didn't seem right. Who was the third guy?

My need to get off of the toll plaza made me decide to take a chance. I threw my pack into the rear seat and vaulted into the open convertible.

As I settled in, the driver put the top up on the car and pulled toward the toll booth. After we passed the toll collector, Sean turned around and held up a can of beer.

"How about a cold one?"

The guy to my left jerked upright. "Beer? Sure."

"Yeah, man," I said. "It's hot out there."

Sean turned back to the front. I heard a can hiss open and then a second one. It took a few seconds before the man handed the beer over his shoulder, first to the curly-headed guy then to me.

The beer was cold, and we both downed it fast. "Bridge Over Troubled Waters" wafted from the radio. The driver said something I couldn't make out. Suddenly, I was drowsy and felt like puking.

I woke up in a perfectly still, stifling-hot car. The sun was low in the west. The curly headed guy was passed out in the seat next to me. My pack was nowhere in sight.

I poked him. "Hey, wake up."

Nothing.

I poked him harder. "Wake up!"

His head shot up and he waved his arms. "What? What? What?" He looked at me, then toward the front seat. "Where the fuck are we?"

"I don't know. Where are your friends?"

"I dunno." The man rubbed his face. "They picked me up just before you."

"You didn't know them? Where's my pack?"

"Beats me." He shook his head as if to clear it, then turned to look out the rear window. The trunk lid stood open. "Aw, no. My pack was in the trunk. They got my shit. Aw, man. They got my shit."

He lurched forward, grabbing for the door handle, shoved against the back side of the front seat and fell out the door, tumbling onto gravel. He scrabbled up and peered into the open trunk, picked up a backpack, turned it upside down and shook it. Empty. He threw it on the ground and paced back and forth behind the car.

I slid over and climbed out.

Curly-headed guy was about 5'11". His dirty jeans covered scuffed engineer boots with rusty buckles. A gray t-shirt stretched over a beer belly and his fingernails were black with grease.

The Cutlass was parked at the edge of a large gravel lot bordered by tall weeds growing up through the carcasses of rusty pickups and school buses. Gas pumps stood fifty yards off. A rusty sign read, "Mel's Super Service." The breeze had died. A swarm of gnats floated silently in the waning sunlight.

My head hurt, my hands trembled. I spied my pack in the front seat, my clothes a heap on the floor. I opened the passenger side door. "At least they left my stuff." I crammed my dirty clothes back into the pack. "They need to come back for the car."

My fellow passenger leaned on the left rear quarter panel. "Probly not. It's stolen."

"Why do you say that?" I asked.

"Look, dumbass." He pointed.

A tangle of wires hung below the dash under the steering wheel. Bile burned my throat. I had been kidnapped in a hot-wired car and left at a no-name gas station in a remote place with a population of two. Guessing by the sun, we'd been passed out for at least five hours. I didn't know what town I was in, or even what state.

I was dizzy and leaned against the car to regain my balance.

What do I do now? I stuck my hand into my pocket and felt crumpled dollar bills. Three bucks. On a dead, two-lane blacktop. And the sun was going down. A flood of panic made me dizzy.

I slid down the car and landed heavily on the gravel.

"What's your name?" the guy asked.

"Nate."

"I'm Spider."

Spider slid down next to me. The stink of stale sweat drifted from him. He pulled a pack of Camels out of his jeans. "Man, this is some bad spot." His head sagged. "Well, let that be a lesson," he mumbled. He lit up a smoke and took a drag.

"What?" I asked.

"My friend Norma used to say that when I was little, whenever I did stupid stuff and got hurt like jumpin' off a porch roof or riding a bike with no brakes."

That sounded like something my mother would have said, as if I was supposed to know how life worked. Just how was I supposed to know? No one ever told me anything until it was too late. "What'd they steal from you?"

He raised his head and stared at me, then sighed. "They stole $2000 worth of top-shelf bennies."

I knew what bennies were because several of my friends used them. I had long hair and tried to act all cool, but I never used the drugs that were always around, except for weed. A lot of my friends used speed. They used downers, too. A couple of them had tried heroin. One died within six months, the other was just gone. I lumped all "hard" drugs together. Bennies included.

I stood. "I gotta get going."

Spider lifted his head and squinted as he looked at me. "Where to?"

I looked left, then right. My eyes settled on the two-lane blacktop that ran in front of the gas station. "I dunno. Can't stay here. What if they catch us with that stolen car?"

Spider tossed the butt of his cigarette and pulled off his right boot. A clear baggie fell onto the gravel. "Sons a bitches didn't get my cash." A stack of bills showed through the bag. "I got about four hunnert. How much you got?"

I looked around again, then back to Spider. "Some."

Spider put his boot back on and got up. He grinned, revealing a missing tooth. "Aw, it's all right if you're broke." He held a ten-dollar bill out. "I'll spot ya ten."

I wanted that money, but this guy was a drug dealer. Who knew what his motives were. And I'd ridden here in a stolen car. I could wind up in jail; all things my mother constantly warned me about. I kept looking at the ten-dollar bill and thought about the three bucks in my pocket. But I didn't move.

"You'll take it eventually." He pocketed the money.

The metallic rumble of an overhead door sounded across the empty lot. A man walked towards us, wiping his hands on a red shop towel. I reached into the front seat of the Cutlass and grabbed my pack, intending to walk away.

"Too late now, brother," Spider said. He walked to the trunk and started stuffing what remained of his things into his backpack.

"You guys still here?" the man asked as he approached. A patch on his coveralls read "Charlie."

I looked at Spider.

He shrugged. "Oh, yeah. We're still here."

"Your two pals used my phone a couple of hours ago. Somebody came and picked 'em up. Said you was gonna stay with the car. You need repairs, or gas or somethin'?"

"That's okay, Charlie. No, we're not in need of anything. We just, ah, needed to rest a little before we took off."

"Well, you fellas take care then. I need to get going." Charlie headed back toward the garage.

"Hey buddy," Spider said. "What town is this?"

"Warren, Pennsylvania."

"Is there a diner here?"

Charlie nodded.

"Them guys took the keys, so we're sorta stuck. Could we catch a ride with you?"

The mechanic pulled a watch out of his pocket. "If you hurry up and get your stuff, I just got time to drop you."

Spider grabbed his pack and slammed the trunk closed. "Let's go," he said and walked after the man. Not a single car passed since Spider and I had come to. I felt tired and a little sick. As iffy as he was, Spider seemed like my best bet at the moment, so I followed him to Charlie's old pickup and climbed in.

Charlie let us out on the main street of Warren in front of the only place that was lit up. The sign on the door read, "Open 'til midnight seven days a week." The Finer Diner was long and narrow with a few tables and a lunch counter. The place was empty except for a gray-haired man wearing a stained white apron, standing behind the counter scraping the grill.

We took a table and ordered coffee. The clock on the back wall read 8:30.

The man in the apron set down two steaming mugs. "You gonna eat?"

"No, just coffee for me," I said.

"You *are* broke, aren't you?" Spider said.

"I have a few bucks."

Spider looked at me and then at the cook. "Bring me three eggs over easy with bacon and American fries. And toast. With lots of butter." He looked back at me and grunted. "And bring this sad sack the same thing."

I hadn't eaten since the night before. I didn't protest.

We sat sipping coffee, the restaurant quiet except for the clanging of the cook's spatula on the iron grill. The aroma of bacon and potatoes frying made my stomach burn with hunger.

Spider's forearms rested on the tabletop. His eyelids sagged. I was tired, too, but couldn't relax. My mother's voice ran around in my head, gaining momentum with every lap. *"How do you get into these messes? Why don't you think first? Can't you stay away from trouble? Now you're stuck with this criminal and you don't even know where you are."*

"Shut *up!*" I hollered and slammed my hand on the tabletop.

The grill man spun around and stared. Spider jerked back in his chair and almost fell over. "What the hell?"

Heat rose in my face. I hunched over and stared at the table's scarred surface. "I'm not crazy," I mumbled even though I felt like I was.

The spatula clanked and scraped for another minute, then the man appeared at our table and set down full plates.

Spider shoveled a pile of potatoes into his mouth, ignoring me.

I dug in, too.

After he finished his food he leaned back and lit a cigarette.

"Man, you are some changeable son of a bitch. I don't know whether to feel sorry for you or be afraid."

"Why would you be scared of me? I've been getting my ass kicked since I was in grade school. I get over-whelmed sometimes and stuff leaks out. But you're a drug dealer, and who knows what else. I should be afraid of you."

"You need to keep your voice down." Spider leaned his elbows on the table and whispered, "Hmph. Drug dealer. That's a laugh. I don't have any drugs for sale at the moment. But, I see what you're sayin', with them assholes stealing the bennies from me and all. I guess that makes me seem like a drug dealer."

Leaning back, I studied the miles on Spider's face. He appeared about thirty, but it was hard to tell. There were scars and gouges that said he'd been around a while.

"Sold everythin' I had, even my Harley. I didn't wanna borrow money, and for sure I didn't want any partners. I had $2500 and a plan. But that's all done with now."

"So, you're not a drug dealer?"

"Not hardly." He mashed the end of his cigarette into the ashtray and leaned back. "I feel like a repeat dumbass. I get great ideas, then hold on to them until they explode all over me. It's a wonder I'm still alive."

Young Adult Novel Excerpt
Final Judge—S.R. Staley
Tallahassee, Florida

First Place—*History will Dissolve Me*
Michael Pesant—Asheville, North Carolina

Elijah kept mentioning the Egg McMuffin, like that was the part of my story that mattered.

"You're gonna regret it," he said. "The food here sucks."

Fifty-three days into the program, Elijah claimed to be nearing graduation. He smelled like my dad's old fish tank, the one no one bothered to clean until we found its inhabitants floating belly-up. I wouldn't be staying here long enough to eat the food, let alone fifty days.

Earlier that morning, at the airport McDonald's, they'd bought me breakfast, but I'd only drank the coffee, leaving the bag of food to fester on the plane. I'd lost my appetite when I overheard one of the men on their cellphone, reassuring my mother that I was about to eat. These same men crashed into my bedroom late the night before, barking like drill instructors, and pressed a brochure into my hands for a program three states away, a wilderness camp for troubled teens.

"They *gooned* you," Elijah translated into program kid slang. "That's how everyone gets here. Your parents pay them a stack to transport you. Double, if you fight or run."

I'd arrived at the camp in the backseat of a rental car, counting minutes since the gas station, the last sign of civilization. Unlike the goons, the staff at the program killed with kindness, invariably polite and empathetic, even as they strip-searched me. The few words that escaped my mouth they listened to and reflected back, bundled in agreement and validation, like the sweetest mirrors in the world.

"I hear you're feeling tired and confused," said Lyle, one of the agreeing machines, a stout woodland creature, layered in plaid and synthetic fleece. "Who wouldn't be, after what you've been through?"

I knew a trap when I saw one.

I *could* react honestly, which is to say, freak the fuck out, and they'd conclude I was sick, in desperate need of this so-called therapy; or alternately, play it cool, like always, and end up taking one compliant step at a time, down a path cut for someone else.

I tried to keep my mouth shut, a strategy, but mostly by default, paralyzed between two bad choices.

Of course, mutism is probably listed in the manual of psychiatric disorders, too.

I allowed myself one request, a phone call home.

"You want to call your parents, to ask if there's been a mistake," Lyle said, "hundred percent understandable.

A cloud lifted. My mom wouldn't leave me here. I'd missed my chance to convince her the night before, not wanting to risk a fight that might wake my grandmother. "We can't keep ignoring the problem, Moses," she'd said, as the goons ordered me out the door.

"Unfortunately," Lyle apologized, tugging his beard, "I'm just an instructor. You have to ask your therapist about a call."

This burned, but I didn't let Lyle see me seethe. I hated this therapist already, knew before meeting him he couldn't help. Who decided I needed a therapist? Why could he deny me a phone? Didn't people in jail get a phone call?

"When is my, um, this therapist coming?" I asked.

"I know it's frustrating he isn't here," he said. "I'll page him."

"Thanks," I forced out. "What about my shoes?"

"You have to ask him that, too."

They'd locked up my possessions upon arrival. I hadn't brought much, but they even took my clothes, replacing them with "field gear." Lyle spent the morning encouraging me to initial everything with a Sharpie, but I couldn't acknowledge these strange garments as mine: the scratchy quick-dry shirts, nylon hiking pants, Walmart boxers, waterproof socks, rubber thong sandals.

My feet froze in the sandals. When I joined "my" group on the trail, Lyle explained, I'd get a pair of boots. I just wanted my sneakers. The base camp was plenty wilderness for me: two cabins and a set of trailers functioning as staff offices, separated from the road by a fast-moving creek. Elijah was the only other patient I'd met. Two girls and a female staff occupied the other cabin, but per Lyle we wouldn't mix, program rules. They'd scattered the rest of the inmates throughout the adjoining forest; base camp reserved for newbies or those requiring medical attention.

"Want to see my toe?" Elijah asked, peeling back yellowed layers of bandage.

I didn't.

They'd confiscated my watch, but when Lyle handed out peanut butter tortillas, I sensed noon. Citing no appetite, I passed, a move denounced by Elijah as a rookie mistake. Lyle charted my skipped lunch as a "meal refusal," as if the paperwork absolved him if I starved. Soon after, the therapist arrived. He looked like a ten-year-older version of Lyle: balding and paunchier, but cleaner, his flannel shirt tucked into khakis instead of hanging loose over trail pants.

"Moses?"

I nodded.

"Colin." He extended a hand, and I noticed he was married, or at least still wore a ring. "Can we go through this assessment?" he asked, waggling a clipboard.

"I was told you could arrange a phone call."

Colin looked down at his shoes. "Why don't we sit somewhere and talk?"

"Here's fine," I said, making space on the cabin steps, the closest point to civilization, since the trailers were off limits to patients.

"Let's sit by the creek," he said. "I get tired of these stuffy cabins."

"Your call."

Colin grabbed two sleeping pads off a stack on the cabin porch. "Butt pads," he explained, "so we don't freeze our asses - literally."

He laughed, and waited, but I only reached for the pad. I knew I should laugh at his jokes, but my face betrayed me. Before walking away, Colin consulted Lyle.

"Keep eyes," he ordered. "He may run."

"I can't call my mom?" I clarified a few minutes later, swallowing my incredulity.

"It's not part of the program," Colin said, further shifting responsibility. "Not at first—patients work through phases before earning a call."

"Earn?" My voice cracked, despite myself. "Isn't it a fundamental right?"

"I hear you're frustrated about earning a call."

32

Losing it, I threw the jail thing at him, but stopped to breathe, recognizing myself on the verge, pulling out of the spiral.

"Don't worry," he laughed. "This isn't jail."

Worse, I thought.

"What if my parents want to call me, they can't?"

"They can," he said. "They're your parents."

"How? Do they even know where I am?"

"We let them know you arrived safe."

This didn't feel safe. I was teetering, and Colin could tell. He kept glancing toward Lyle.

"Maybe you'd like to write them a letter?"

"Like through the mail?"

"No," he laughed, pausing for me to laugh and stiffening when I didn't. "We scan them to email."

"If I write them asking to call, you'll send it now?"

"I'll scan it to them," he said, then squared his shoulders towards me. "But first we finish this assessment, understand?"

We sat on the butt pads while Colin assessed me, probing for emotional soft spots: fodder for treatment. I cooperated, but envisioned some imaginary lawyer encouraging me to offer as little information as necessary, to avoid incriminating myself.

Why was I sent here? No idea.

Did I feel depressed? Now.

Had I ever considered hurting myself, or someone else? No. I didn't mention the airplane, where I'd prayed for every rumble of turbulence to devolve into something bigger.

Once assessed, I returned to the cabin. Colin said he'd be back for my letter.

"Take your time," he said, and left before I could protest.

Lyle provided paper, lined dark for easy scanning, with spaces to list my group name, therapist, phase, days spent in the program. If I left them blank, I risked looking insolent, or sloppy, but when I filled them in, I felt manipulated, my independence violated.

Mom,

You need to call me before it's too late. I've suffered enough. I don't need this, too. This program won't help.

Trust me,

Moses

I waited forever for Colin to collect my letter, trying not to ask Lyle too often when he'd be back.

"I hear you're frustrated," Lyle said. "He'll be back."

I couldn't sit still, and as I paced the space between cabins and creek, Lyle became concerned.

"Wilderness seems scary," he said, "But once you realize you can survive here, you can face whatever's eating you back home."

This was a theme; Colin, Lyle, the goons, even Elijah all assumed I feared the woods, but they had it backwards.

At Lyle's urging, Elijah demonstrated fire-building for me, sweating and grunting as he muscled a tiny ember into life with a set of sticks he called a bow drill. I wondered if they knew Bic lighters cost a dollar and lasted forever.

Elijah hissed at me when Lyle walked out of earshot.

"You get high?"

I shrugged.

"Me too," he said. "But listen, if you plan to keep doing drugs, you need to chill. Learn how to do your time."

I stared at him, thinking.

"This is my fourth program," he added. "You sure you don't want to see my toe?"

As the sun receded behind the cabins, Colin reappeared. "Good news," he announced to no one in particular.

"My phone call?"

"You can join your group," he continued. "They aren't far – couple miles, I'll get your boots."

"My letter," I said, thrusting it at him.

He read it without asking.

"You said you'd scan it."

"I will," he said, eyeing Lyle.

"I'll wait."

"Wouldn't you rather join your group?"

"Please," I begged.

Colin walked away, and soon Lyle came around with a pot of lentils and mouthful of encouragement. I accepted a half-portion, for his sake, two steaming ladles of mush dropped into a ceramic mug.

"Whatever you don't eat," Elijah squealed, "you have to carry for a week – it's called a natural consequence."

Colin returned, quicker this time. He sat down next to me before he let me see my mother's emailed response. I sensed him coordinating with Lyle while I read, gaming out my reaction.

"Bullshit."

"I hear you're—"

"You don't hear shit."

"It's time to face this, Moses," he said, quoting my Mom's email.

"This won't solve anything. I need to call her!"

"She's not ready to talk yet—she needs you to work this program."

My self-control slipping, I pulled Colin deeper down the spiral with each successive argument. I accused him of lying, manipulation, child abuse.

"Want me to level with you?" he countered, a new edge to his voice. "You weren't going to have a phone call – I just went through the motions to give you time to adjust."

"You're forcing me to do this? That's the lesson—I never had a choice?"

"You have infinite choices," Colin said, easing back into his therapist voice.

"You've been making them all day, even when you think you haven't."

"I don't get it."

"You do," he said. "Now your turn to level with me—why are you really here?"

I felt something unravel, and my perception flit around the camp like a live wire. To the left of the cabin, a trail disappeared into the woods. In front, Lyle carefully rewrapped Elijah's toe. The heavy mug of lentils started to burn my fingers, and I eyed the road, just beyond the control of Colin's bullshit grin. I surveyed my choices and readied for the contact. I wouldn't regret another meal.

It's funny how so many lies can build up inside until you almost start to wear them like a patch of stubble on your neck or a stain on your shirt. The big ones you absorb so completely you almost forget or start to believe them yourself. But then the little things start to add up and bother you; you begin living with a certain amount of paranoia, constantly checking yourself in the mirror, cupping your palm over your mouth and nose to smell your own breath, tucking in errant shirt tails . . . It's as if your appearance becomes the dike holding back oceans of deceit and you are constantly surveying for leaks.

It was halfway through seventh period that day when I rounded the corner of the East Building with trepidation, scared to run into Brother Angelo or Mr. McEwan. Those two were Headmaster and Dean of Discipline, respectively, though they were both dicks. We were only a week into March but already it was hot as shit. The swampy South Florida air was melting the Dep brand #7 Super-Hold hair gel that was keeping my hair slicked back and within dress code length compliance. Just last month McEwan had snuck up behind me, grabbed a handful, and jerked me out of the lunch line.

"This is shabby, Mendoza," he'd said, wiping a gel covered hand down the front of my shirt. "Don't look like this tomorrow."

Hiding long hair with a slicked back gel job was small potatoes around here. A senior named Ernie Diaz had a tongue piercing, and as a result couldn't really open his mouth during school hours. Not that Ernie had much to say in class. Small potatoes or not, I had no desire for Disciplinary Detention—an hour after school standing face up against the office wall— and was relieved to step into the frosty air of the guidance conference room without incident. It was like that here, all about appearances. You could be a murderer, and no one would give a shit as long as your hair was short, your shirt tucked in, and your face free from any visible signs of weirdness or rebellion.

I was out of class to undergo the sacrament of confession, a monthly ritual for all students here at

Christopher Columbus Catholic High School For Boys. This was not your standard daytime TV confession. There was no black box in which to kneel and spill your deepest secrets anonymously to a shadow priest behind dark screen. Instead, we went face to face across grainy fake wooden boardroom table in the antartically air-conditioned conference room with Brother Eladio, who moonlighted as the school's librarian. As the assigned confessor for juniors last names A-P, Brother Eladio served as the Catholic School equivalent to a guidance counselor. As an 80-plus year old (I'm guessing, but he was fucking old) lifetime monk with limited command of spoken English, he was about as well suited to the job of relating to 17-year-old Miami boys as my Cuban great-grandmother Chichi was to being the lead guitarist of a thrash metal band.

I have to admit though, he had his routine down. Often, after school at Pedro or Rudy's house, we'd sit across the card table in his backyard and take turns playing Brother Eladio. Of course he started with the standard confession business of opening prayer of contrition and admission of time passed since last confessing (always exactly one month), but then he'd jump into the Holy Trinity of teenage transgression with a shocking and often giggle inducing (but don't you dare) matter-of-factness.

"Do jou dreenk?"

"No, Brother Eladio"

"Do jou yoose drogs?"

"No, Brother." I'd reply, grinding teeth at this point to suppress the impulse to laugh.

"Do jou mastoorbate?"

Once you were found not guilty of the major sins, the line of questioning tended towards a more proactive destination, i.e., what you've done good instead of the bad things you haven't done.

"And how have jou glorified the Lor this month by serving others?"

I found myself suddenly drained of the desire to lie to men of the cloth.

"To tell the truth, Brother, I haven't really done much.

"Well then, Moses, jou mus go and serve others in the name of jor Lor."

Later that night, I was practicing analogies in my SAT prep book when Pedro Rodriguez beeped me with a 420-911. My parents were watching the news in the den, but looked over suspiciously when they heard the jingle of car keys in my hand.

"I'm gonna go put some gas in the Explorer so I don't have to stop on the way to school tomorrow," I said, hoping that they wouldn't notice that I'd used the same line two nights earlier. Dad hit the mute button and looked at me with wrinkled brow, but Mom beat him to the punch. Their decision making was like that, a first-come, first-served basis.

"Wear your seatbelt, Moses," she said, draining the watery remains of her wine glass.

Pedro lived about twenty blocks away in a gated enclave of wealthy South Americans called Andalusian Oaks. I did wear my seatbelt too, as I raced down US-1 to make a twenty-block pot deal look like a five-block trip to the Shell Station. I was pissed when I got to the guard gate and found a five-car backup. The gate was a ruse, however, as they lacked the legal ability to restrict people from entering the community and could only slow you down to photograph you license plate numbers.

I didn't even bother with the door when I got there, knowing he'd be out back by the pool. Pedro didn't have to make up lies to his parents to hang out on a school night. I knew little about his parents except that they were rich, from Venezuela, and rarely home. Also Pedro's mom was smoking hot.

Pedro was lying back in a chaise lounge smoking a grit as I made my way around their landscaped backyard, instinctively reaching over the gate to pull the tab and release the door lock.

"What up, Mo?"

Second Place—*Fairy Godfather*
Robert Fogler—Armed Forces Pacific

Franklyn eyed his reflection, exhaled, and unfolded his wings. The only male fairy to develop butterfly-shaped wings in the history of the realm. They towered over his scrawny frame, filling out the rest of the mirror. A violet hue engulfed his room as the last bit of daylight peeked through the curtains and bounced off his wings. Franklyn let out an even deeper exhale at the sight of the glistening iridescence; he gave them a couple flaps, hoping the flutter would provide some change. But he remained special. Or as everyone put it, a "happy accident."

Franklyn's wings sprouted on his eighth birthday: a typically joyous occasion for any young fairy. He could still remember the slight gasp from the crowd as his hindwings emerged and even the sound of the wind as it billowed through their open gapes once his forewings unfurled. Now here he was, the night of his seventeenth birthday, possessing the same special set. Well, not exactly the same; they seemed extra sparkly as his magic continued to grow. Perfect. He circled the empty suitcase on the wooden floor, ignoring the chore. Then he let his wings slump down to their resting position and fell back onto his bed.

A soft knock at his door got him to sit up. "Yeah?"

Franklyn's mother cracked open his bedroom door and peeked her head in through the gap. "Are you all set for tomorrow?"

"Almost," he said, tossing a lone sock into the suitcase.

His mother pushed the door open further and stepped in, bringing in a whiff of simmering stew with her. She was clearly in the middle of his birthday dinner. Her red and gold floral apron was tied tightly around her petite figure, and there were a few new additions to the usual food stains. Pinned up in an unruly bun, her dusty blonde hair fought to dangle free. Crooked reading glasses sat in front of her misty blue eyes; their use was mainly for show as she had memorized her recipes a long time ago.

"You don't have to go if you don't want to." She picked up the pile of shirts next to him and took their spot. Her hand gently combed back a few strands of his silver hair.

"What else would I do?"

"You could stay here and help around the farm."

He stared at space left in the suitcase. "I don't have environmental magic."

The Kepler's had been Environmental fairies for generations. Simple wings the color of pale honey or dried grass. When Franklyn's wings developed, his family might have been able to look past the female form. However, there was no denying their color: purple. He was clear on the other side of the spectrum from them.

"So? Magic isn't everything. A lot of the work could be done manually."

"Mom."

"You always complain about being too skinny." She lightly pinched his bicep. "It could help you build some muscle."

"Mom." He half smiled as he pulled his arm away.

"And . . ." She wrapped her arms around Franklyn and pulled him into her, keeping a good grip on him as he resisted. "You would get to be home with your loving mother, who could cuddle you and cradle you and kiss you and hug you every day."

"Alright. Alright. I get it." They were roughly the same size, but Franklyn still managed to peel himself out of her hug. He picked up another sock and threw it at the first one.

Franklyn's mother mimicked him and tossed in one too. "We will at least go tomorrow and meet with Headmistress Aster. If you decide that you don't want to go there, we will figure something out. Sound like a plan?"

"Yea. That's fair."

"Okay. Now finish packing because dinner is almost ready." She stood up and dropped the pile of shirts into the suitcase.

"Mom." His call caught her just before she reached the door.

"Yes?"

He rubbed his palms against the bed quilt and stayed staring at the growing suitcase community. "I'm sorry."

"For what, son?"

"You know."

She stepped back over to him. Her fingertips raised his chin up, forcing him to look at her. "Apologize when you say something wrong. Apologize when you do something wrong. But never apologize for who you are. Do you hear me?"

"Yes."

"Don't let anyone tell you who or what you need to be. You are you." Her thumb wiped away the faint glimmer of tears from his eyes. She kissed his forehead and headed back to the door. "You are my son. Whatever you decide tomorrow, I will support you. Okay?"

"Okay."

"Love you."

"Love you too, mom."

She was almost out the door when she turned around and smiled. "Oh, I forgot to mention, I heard that the Creer family's son is coming back home. You remember the Creers; they live just down the street. Well, their son is studying medical magic at Pladarian but has decided to do fieldwork this term. Gertie showed me a picture of him, very handsome. He's a couple years older than you, but she was pretty sure he was single."

"Oh my gosh, mom."

"I'm just letting you know what I heard. You could stay and meet him." Her cadence floated into a jest. "Maybe spend the term together. And then I would have two sons to love and—"

"Mom!"

Franklyn grabbed a pile of clothes and threw it at her. She was too quick, and they bounced off the door as she shut it.

"Finish packing," She said as she popped her head in from behind the door and looked at the scattered clothes. "And clean your room while you're at it. I want to use it as a pantry when you're away."

He knew there was no way she could bring herself to change his room. And besides that, it was already clean. Except for the thrown pants, it was always clean. Franklyn didn't have enough room for messes or clutter. He only had a bed, dresser, and bookcase, but his grandpa had built them to scale for the normal male Kepler. Their dark, ornate bulk overpowered his tiny room, but they always made him feel grand.

Franklyn got off the bed, gathered up the pants from the floor, and folded them into the suitcase. He stepped over to his bookcase and glanced through the titles, trying to find the right one to bring. *Creatures of the Mayvian*

Realms. What Can Be Domesticated. Non-Magical Beings. The engraved butterflies fluttered as he ran his finger across the shelves; a nice touch his grandpa added. When he reached the bottom shelf, he noticed a couple of his mother's books poorly hidden on the ends.

"Mom?" He yelled through the door. "Did you put cookbooks on my bookcase?"

There was a bit of contemplative silence before his mother finally answered. "Dinner's ready!"

The Keplers were not morning fairies. After a rushed breakfast, Franklyn and his mother flew across their fields towards the Godmother Academy. He let the smell of the harvested hay wash over him as he drifted close to the barrels. As much as he was going to miss harvest time, he was ready for the opportunity to try his magic. To at least be with the same color of fairies.

The Elders had kept a close eye on Franklyn while he was growing up, documenting any changes to his wings. But this year it became clear there would be no variation from the color purple. The color of Godmother magic. And because his magic would grow stronger, the Elders reluctantly agreed for him to attend the academy. Another first for the realm.

It took twenty minutes of Franklyn's mother insisting manual labor on their farm built more than muscle before they landed in front of the Godmother Academy: an average cottage in the middle of Penwood Forest. The mossy-stoned building was surrounded by a wildflower infested clearing. Smoke furled up from its squatty chimney as overly joyful birds hopped through the billows.

"So this is it." Franklyn kicked away some of the weeds scratching through the gaps of his sandals.

"It's so—"

"Quaint."

"Charming," Franklyn's mother continued, ignoring the flatness in his tone. "I'm sure it's enchanted."

"I hope so." The pine mixed with the prickling scent of wildflowers curled up his nose.

"Our house is bigger than this."

"Well, it's not too late to go back."

"We're not going back."

"Then quit sulking and knock."

He followed the trail of sprinkled pebbles up to the wooden door and gave it a timid knock. There was a short and hollow echo before the door flung open.

"Goodness me!" A set of short plump arms wrapped themselves around Franklyn and pulled him into a tight bear-hug. The pudgy woman behind them gave him a jiggle. "You must be Franklyn Kepler! I'm so happy you decided to come!"

With a burly chuckle, the woman set him down and let him go. Franklyn quickly took a couple steps back, making sure she couldn't reach him again. She was a little shorter than he was, maybe only five feet tall. But an off-center brunette beehive provided an additional foot. It was messily woven with pieces of gold tinsel and strands of grey hair.

"Oh, this is so exciting." Her cheeks took over her round face as she smiled. A faint twinkle in her brown eyes winked over her cheekbones. "My goodness . . . I am getting ahead of myself."

She stepped back slightly, still blocking the entrance, and a warm peachy glow fell upon her like spotlight.

Despite the heavy embellishments of pearls and beads, her rose gold ball gown stayed lackluster. She gave it a brush over, causing a few beads to shake loose and tumble to the ground. Another chuckle. A pink opal wand shot out of her sleeve into her hand. It let a wimpy poof of glitter from its crooked tip; she raised it into the air and did a couple twirls. The tulle of her dress tripled in size with the spins and squashed his suitcase into him. Franklyn took another large step back, unsure of how much more space she might need.

"I'm Godmother Torble," she said, stopping just shy of dizziness. She gave a bow and a curtsy that came across as more of a bop. "Advisor for first year students. Oh, we are going to have so much fun together. Well, sort of together. I was just so excited to meet you. We've never had so many special students before. Any special student really. Unless you count Godmother Yvette. But I don't know if allergies are really the same as your situation. They were fairly severe though."

"Delightful." Franklyn smiled as sincerely as he could muster up. He'd much rather be called an outcast and avoid the social politeness.

His mother stepped up behind him and tried to peer into the cottage. "Mrs. Tor—"

"Godmother."

"Godmother Torble, I'm Franklyn's mother, Lorna, and he is supposed to be meeting with the headmistress soon. Would you mind showing us where to go?"

"Certainly, dear. Certainly." She did several quick hops, causing more beads to fall and her dress to shrink back to normal.

Franklyn shifted his suitcase to his left hand. He was starting to regret bringing *The Complete List of Magically*

Capable Creatures, 476th Edition. It was the most worn book of his collection, and despite its weight, it held the essence of his room in its pages. Although, a travel size version wouldn't be a bad thing to have. He brought the suitcase back to his right and propped it up with his knee.

"Let me get that for you." Godmother Torble pointed her wand at his suitcase. "In this suitcase is all the stuff that Franklyn brings. So help us out and give it wings!"

Swirls of burgundy fairy dust flowed out from her wand and floated over to Franklyn; it was accompanied by the comforting aroma of apple pie. Franklyn's face lit up as he inhaled deeply; he had never seen godmother magic in person before. The other magic types didn't have smells or require the enhancement of fairy dust. He watched as the dust circled around the suitcase and lifted it out of his hand into the air. It swarmed over the handles and flickered. As the dust dissipated, the handles morphed into a pair of brown, feathery wings.

One of the wings had manifested bent, and it was difficult for the suitcase to stay airborne. It flopped on the ground like a fish, before it was finally able to stop upright. Having found its bearings, it flew up at them and tried to make its way into the cottage. They ducked as it missed every time and banged into the frame. Unsuccessful, the suitcase backed away from the door. It drooped and swayed from the struggle to keep flying.

"I'm really okay with carrying myself," Franklyn said as he swatted for his suitcase. Before he could almost grab it, it suddenly propelled itself up above the cottage and immediately dropped into the chimney.

Godmother Torble waved them along as she made her way into the cottage. "Don't worry. I'm sure it will find us."

They stepped through the door and found themselves on the outskirts of another forest. Across a narrow meadow of snowdrop flowers stood the formidable academy: an oversized cottage. Ten stories built from a mixture of faded bricks and stones; their weathered browns and greys accented by levels of uneven windows and swooping thatched roofs. Dark iron sconces dotted the façade, providing anchors for the intrusive vines that already covered a majority of the building.

There were no visible suns in the sky, yet the world held a midday glow. Franklyn looked back at the door they came through; it was embedded into the trunk of a thick birch tree. Judging by the lack of suns and nonnative birch, Franklyn knew they were no longer in their homeland, Orchathyst.

His mother leaned over to him. "I told you it would be enchanted."

"Of course it's enchanted! We're godmothers!" Godmother Torble raised her arms up towards the academy as she sang her statements. But she only brought them halfway up before pausing. "Although, it was actually Professor Beril who created this, um, this semi-dimensional world. She can explain it better. She's a blue fairy and the first-year realm instructor. Oh, you'll love her. Been with the academy for ages. Since it opened. She just keeps going, no matter how many times she gets lost."

"Can't wait." Despite his sarcastic tone, a part of Franklyn was genuinely excited at the prospect of exploring other realms. He had always admired blue fairies and their ability to open portals and travel to different worlds. Discovering and documenting new things.

"First things first." Torble turned and skipped back to the door. "If you are expecting any guests, including your parents, you must register them with Flec. Only registered guests are able to enter the academy. If they are not registered, they will walk into this."

Godmother Torble clapped her hands, and the forest around them disappeared. They were now standing in the drab interior of a cottage. A thick layer of dust rested upon the spare furnishings, and long spider webs tethered them together. A table and set of flimsy chairs. A drooping cot. And a moldy chest. On the far wall, a mirror reflected the orange glow of the smoldering logs in the fireplace.

Through the windows, Franklyn's mother could see they were back in their home realm.

"You better not forget to register me."

Franklyn crossed his arms and shrugged, giving her a smirk. "I'll try and remember."

"Yes! You need to remember! Not registered: you see this. Registered and   then . . ." Torble said as she clapped again, bringing them back to the academy. She waved her hand at the mirror that was now hanging on a tree. "You'll find Flec somewhere over there."

The expressive face of an old man popped up on the mirror. His wrinkles bunched together as he gave a toothless grin. "Hello there! Welcome to Orc—"

"Oh, we should really get you to your meeting." Torble lifted her skirt and gave herself a running start as she flew off towards the academy.

Realizing Torble wasn't going to wait, Franklyn and his mother quickly followed. They did their best to ignore and dodge the tiny puffs of burgundy fairy dust that appeared behind her.

"I can do more than register!" Flec's shouts grew faint.

Once at the arched entry of the academy, Godmother Torble hovered. Her stubby wings did their best to keep her off the ground as she waited for Franklyn and his mother.

"Alright! Here we are." She pointed upwards. "Franklyn, just make your way up to the top, and you'll find the headmistress office on the roof. And Mrs. Kepler, the waiting area is just right inside these doors. If either of you get turned around, just ask the furniture for directions."

"Thank you so much," his mother said.

"Of course, dear." Torble floated forward and cupped the side of Franklyn's cheek. She peered into his eyes. "I do hope you decide to attend. Now go. And I'll go see where your suitcase wandered off to."

As Torble puttered off, Franklyn's mother batted away some of the burgundy dust balls.

"Do you still want to go through with this?"

"I think I'm ready to find out what I'm capable of." Franklyn said as he looked up the building. "I mean, I already have pretty good cadence."

"You don't need an academy to tell you what you're capable of." His mother reached out and held his hand, getting him to look back at her. "I know you can do anything you set your mind to; you just need to figure it out on your own."

Third Place—Warmth
Rachel Bean—Tinley Park, Illinois

The egg was given to me when I was eight by my Uncle Stefan.

Uncle Stefan was always bringing us unusual things. Boats with wheels, cooled lava, sparkling stones, or cloth in many colors from some far away land. Ever since I could remember, I'd gotten odd baubles from my Uncle, but they were so much more than *things* to me.

When I was eleven, I had created a makeshift shelf out of a board my papa hadn't needed when he was building the second floor of our home. It was a dark piece of wood with several knots that he hadn't liked the look of, so I decided to make use of it.

I nudged a rag into the crevices of a wheeled boat, which had miraculously maintained its robust color even ten years later. The azure blue of the body hadn't faded a shade and I had meticulously cleaned the decorative white parts each week so they didn't yellow. I pulled the rag along the cord attached to the aft before settling the novelty back in its place. Everything else simply needed a run over—the lava, the stones, the glass flower required more meticulous attention, but mostly I was done.

That just left the egg.

I crouched down, gathering my skirts to the side so the ground wouldn't dirty them further, and carefully lifted the wooden box to survey the gleaming jade oval. It neither gathered dust nor dulled, even without any special sort of attention. I rested my hand on the top crest and it brought back the smell of worldliness, of dirt and pine, of spicy smoke. It was my favorite gift from Uncle Stefan, whom I hadn't seen in over five years now.

"Kitten, you're eight years old now and I've gotten you something quite special," my Uncle Stefan had said, squatting to hoist the rather large item out of his sack. With him came the sour smell of old pipe tobacco. I breathed it in deep. Uncle Stefan always smelled different every time he showed up. The places where he'd traveled soaked into his clothing, into his skin, and it made me yearn for the sea and lands far away. The item he pulled from his bag, covered by a pilling brown blanket, brought on another wave of the smoky smell. "You're an intelligent young woman, Kitten, and I do figure you'll appreciate this more than anyone else." He sat down across from me and folded his legs to sit comfortably.

I, myself, had already been perilously perched on my haunches, the backs of my thighs on the heels of my feet. I remember this feeling, despite the eight years that have passed. My family hadn't always been privy to the luxury other people in our neighborhood enjoyed; we'd only recently acquired the land for this house. Our furniture was all hand-made by my mother, who had laboriously upholstered and stuffed the sturdy, reseda green couch herself while I held her materials, setting them in her outstretched hand as directed. It was overstuffed and over sewn, but it was my favorite place to sprawl out and read. It was like most things in our house—made by us, a bit unconventional, but homey. Cozy. Well-loved.

Gifts were a rarity in our lives, especially ones that weren't handmade or necessities. My last "gift" had been a ruffled piece of cloth to add to the bottom of my already well-worn dress so that my ankles were covered. Mama had presented it to me, beaming proudly because it was nearly the exact same shade as the dress it was meant for. I had smiled and petted the cloth and begged her to sew it on right away because I loved it so much.

Uncle Stefan's gifts were different. They rarely had any sort of practical purpose—I had barely known what to do with the glass flower he'd given me a year ago. The stem was so delicately strung out and the petals were curved to fine edges as thin as Papa's sharpest knives. Best of all, though, was the silken bag Uncle Stefan had presented it to me in. It smelled sharp and citrusy and Uncle Stefan told me it was bergamot or neroli, both were used in incense that the Hurakans frequently burned in their shops. I had pressed it to my nose and loved that I was smelling another country, this place I hadn't been, and Uncle Stefan had told me story after story of his time there while I held the pale yellow cloth to my face. I could imagine that I was *there*.

I inhaled this new scent like I had that neroli, but this one was smoky, a little woody, and it filled my nostrils and swirled around my head in tufts.

"It's vetiver." Uncle Stefan's eyes crinkled with his wide smile, seeing me bask in the earthy aroma. "Now, we have to be quick, before your Papa returns." Uncle Stefan slowly pulled the blanket off, revealing a jade green egg larger than my head. It shone with the brilliance of a gem as he held it close to the array of candles littering the table.

"Stefan, what is that?" Mama had slid forward on the couch to better see, bunching up the voluminous swathes of cloth and tucking them to the side, out of her way.

"It's a replica of a *kasaihlia* egg." He tapped the top of it twice, smartly. "Little miss Kitten, here, had asked what I knew about the *kasaihlias* so much the last time I paid a visit that, when I came across this, I absolutely knew I must pass it on to her."

54

I reached out and touched it but jerked away quickly, surprised by the detailed texture. It wasn't rough, but it had the same bumpy surface that bird's eggs do. It was cold and hard but gleamed with life.

"The color is impressive, Stefan. What was it carved from?" Mama touched it as I had, her eyes widening. "The detail is exquisite."

"I'm unsure what it's made of, to be frank. The woman I got it from . . ."

I wasn't paying their conversation much mind — speculations on material weren't of interest to me. I lifted the egg from my Uncle's hands and he let me have it without breaking pace in his exclamation that it could be molten jewels. It was heavy and I nearly dropped it. Visions of the beautiful shell cracking, shattering across our worn wooden floor made me clutch it tightly between my small fingers. Nothing I owned had ever been so beautiful, nor so hated by my Papa.

So much more came with it than that, though, even eight years later.

"Kat, have you readied?"

I vaguely heard Papa's voice from the first floor, but the egg ensnared my attention. My hand, the one resting on it, was warming, as if in an oven. Bizarre. I dropped the rag in my left hand and rested it on the egg's thicker midsection, but it was cool to the touch.

I shook my head. *The sun.* Of course.

"Katarina? Did you hear me?" Papa's voice carried easily to the second floor.

"Yes, coming!" I called back, ripping my palms away from the grooved surface. I gathered my apron and gallies in my arms from the mattress and left. I jammed my feet into the faded black leather as I descended, hopping precariously from one foot to the other as I tripped down the stairs. They were faded at the centers, where they were most used, the same spots where Fuller and I had slid down on our rears as entertainment when we were still the same height.

"How many times . . ." Papa took a deep breath and watched me descend, step by step. His brown trousers were a shade lighter than his vest, which fit snugly around his burgeoning belly. Today, he wore a powder blue shirt Mama had dyed for him. It matched my dress, just like it matched my brother's pants and vest and my mother's apron.

I quickly cinched my own apron around my waist, the ink bottles tucked inside the deep pockets clinking. A cloak was flung over my shoulders.

"Papa, it's so nice out."

"There's a chill in the air. It's not quite summer yet." He settled a cap on his head. "Now, mind your Papa and bundle up."

I shook my head but adjusted the thin brown wool across my shoulders and tied the ribbon neatly at the base of my throat. It was still soft and silky, unlike the rest of the worn material. It scratched my bare arms, rested uncomfortably across my collar bones, and the hood always flopped over my eyes, but I did love the rutty thing.

"Come along, come along." Papa held the door open and I stepped out.

He closed it behind us and ushered me down the trimmed lawn. The sun was rising to the right, blinding me. We walked directly into the bright rays but there was little else to indicate a new day had begun. Wibon Street was always strangely quiet, even during the busiest hours of day. The houses were all uniquely shaped, some single floors but many built up over the past few years. The lawns were all tended and the street was clean. The roadways were especially silent in the early morning, as if the wind dared not ruffle even the grass at this hour lest it wake the slumbering occupants. Respecting that quiet, Papa and I said nothing until people began to speckle the roads as we strolled closer to the center of town.

"Good morning, Charles." Papa placed a hand on my back to nudge me out of the way. He was nothing if not gracious, especially in minor day-to-day interactions.

Charles clasped Papa's hand as he passed, letting go as quickly as he had taken it. "I shall be stopping by within the week for my order, Brian. We shall catch up. Good day."

"Good day, Charles."

Charles waved farewell as he walked away. He was strange. A good kind, but a strange man. Everything he said had the echo of a longer conversation, as if I had simply come in part way.

"Have you heard anything back from the clerk's office?" Papa asked, pulling me quickly through the intersection. There was a horse and carriage riding down it, but they were still at a distance. Vendors from the market had joined us now, some traipsing down the side of the road carrying large loads strung across their backs in rough-hewn bags. Others walked beside their carts hauled by overlarge steeds.

"Not as of yet." I couldn't stop myself from being angered by the question, though I know it had nothing to do with Papa. I cast down my eyes, cheeks warming, but kept my tone bland. I was anxious and desperate and I wished to admit neither.

"You'll always have Mama and me." Papa slid his arm around my shoulders and squeezed me lightly to his side.

The anger flared then dulled, and I nodded, offering him a small, forced smile. He tried to want what I wanted for myself, but he did it grudgingly, and only out of love, not because he actually supported my dreams. I wanted the job at the clerk's office more than most things, but I was at a terrible disadvantage. I had no schooling and I had no husband, therefore I held no title and was little more than a child to the squinty-eyed codgers who had peered down at me over long, sloped noses as I'd spoken candidly about myself, insisting that a self-taught woman could offer a propensity for learning. Their faces, laden with doubt, had registered nothing more than my sex. I could see that. Yet, I still hoped for a chance the way that people in Gravielle proper hoped the price of land would retrogress. It was futile, but it did not stop the glimmer in their hearts, nor in mine.

The houses had grown closer together, the plots of land that held them shrinking the closer we came to the castle. Papa's shop was blessedly at the center of the hustle and bustle of Gravielle proper and we were rarely short of business, having provided the meat for a few dinners that royalty had indulged in. Those had caused quite a stir in Papa. He'd spent hours inspecting meats for fatty veins and ensuring that the thickness of the steaks was exact before having me carefully wrap each piece in stiff, white paper. He had me re-wrap every single one at least twice, using new paper each time. I'd mentioned that I was a colossal waste. He replied that it most certainly was not. It was an honor to provide meat for a royal dinner.

I don't think they compensated us at all, but I'd cut out my own tongue before saying anything about it to Papa.

The castle loomed in the distance after a large patch of green land that held nothing but an illustrious lawn. A singular road, long and swiveling, for no other reason than aesthetics, led from the edge of Gravielle proper to the castle. There were few people who took that road and even fewer who wanted to. If you were on your way to Gravielle Castle, you were either a prisoner or begging for a loan. Neither ended particularly well.

"Ah, Kat." He nudged me and I followed his gaze. A new vendor. At least, neither of us had seen him before. He was a short fellow, skinny except for his stomach, which burgeoned out much farther than Papa's, like a woman with child. His face was clean but splotched with red from exertion. He gripped the edges of the tipped table and managed to hoist it a few inches before it sunk back into the grass.

Papa stepped up on the other side of it and hoisted it clean into the air, righting it with little help from the small man. I pulled out the legs of the table on one side and he kicked out the folded legs to the right, wooden as well, and together we rested it carefully on the side of the street.

"Thank 'ee." His words were nearly all breath. He stretched out a hand to my father, blatantly walking past me to do it. I frowned. Granted, I hadn't done the bulk of the heavy lifting, but a simple *thank 'ee* tossed in my direction would have been appreciated.

"Unwieldy table you've got there," Papa commented.

"'Tis all I've got for the mo'." He looked down at it despondently.

"What are you selling?" I asked. Perhaps I had overlooked boxes of wares or some such.

Horns sounded loudly as the little man opened his mouth. If he said anything, it was drowned out by the trumpets' blast. Far down the road, a carriage was coming, drawn by shire steeds that stood more than sixteen hands tall, all black, all rippling with sweat. The carriage itself was gargantuan; it covered near the whole road. I didn't have to see the emblem on the side, of lightning striking through purple ground, to know whose carriage it was, but the three crowns adorning the front told me which member of the royal family was inside: Prince Cavan. My father dropped dutifully to his knees and lowered his forehead to touch the ground. I didn't like seeing my father in this position. I didn't like seeing anyone prostrate themselves, but especially not my father.

"Kat," Papa ordered.

My knees hit the ground and, in my anger, I jarred one quite painfully. My newly-dyed dress. Dirty from the damned ground, the pretty blue. Slowly I lowered my upper half, bracing myself on the street with my forearms. I kept my forehead a centimeter above the ground. Eyes wide open, I could see what was there. Dirt. Pebbles that had been dragged from hell knows where. Spit. Trash. *Vermin droppings.*

No. I would not *actually* touch my forehead to this scum.

"What are you both doin'?" the little man asked.

The horses' hooves clip-clopping and the clatter from the wheels against the cobblestone grew louder with each passing second and my heart matched their hurried pace, thumping against my breast bone and echoing into my head. My breath was loud and hot with my lips so close to the ground that I could *taste* the stink and I tried to measure my inhales. This was just like every time before. In. Out.

"Get down," Papa snapped suddenly and I looked up to see the little man still standing, watching our behavior with a cocked head and knitted brow. Papa's fervent eyes met mine, anger sparking in them as he hissed my name. "Kat!" He jutted his chin pointedly downward and I quickly did the same, my body trembling as the hooves came to a halt.

"For what reason would—"

Thick black boots thundered past and his words cut off abruptly.

"Cover your ears. Close your eyes." Papa's voice was barely audible. I chose to listen. I jammed my biceps close to my ears and scrunched my eyes shut tightly and I wish that had been enough to block out the pained cries and muffled thuds of fist striking skin, but it was not. Daft man. Why couldn't he listen? Royalty rarely ventured through Gravielle proper; well, up until the past year. Prince Cavan, the youngest son, had been traipsing from one end of town to the other, especially the past few months, but the carriage was rare. Usually it was just him on his large steed with two guards hurriedly trying to keep pace with his manic speed. People spoke of him with an absurd commonality now, but always in hushed tones and always with fading bruises.

Despite this, I'd never seen the man.

Creative Non-Fiction

Final Judge—Patricia Charpentier
Orlando, Florida

First Place—*Picking up the Pieces*
Liz Jameson—Tallahassee, Florida

"I'll drive. The streets are icy, and I have four-wheel drive in case we get stuck," Mimi said, as she and her friend Barby escaped the throng of post-funeral, casserole-bearing friends of the family at the Spruce Street house. The two had been discreet as they changed from their dress clothes into jeans and sweatshirts, and they'd slipped out without being noticed.

"After all, you're doing me a favor by helping out. It would be a lot easier to stay in there and catch up with old friends than do what I'm asking. Least I can do is drive over," Mimi added.

"I sure as hell don't want to stay in there. It's sad and morbid, and what's worse, the church ladies were starting to corner me," Barby said.

Grim faced, the two moved the cleaning supplies in the passenger seat to the back seat, which was already occupied by mops and a bucket. Barby hunkered down into her parka and adjusted the heat vent, cursing under her breath that it was only late October and they were sure to be in for a mean winter. She'd come down from Jackson Hole for the funeral, so she'd already experienced two months of real cold and was in the first stage of cabin fever, with warm weather seven or eight months away. She stared out the window and saw the sparse, determined trees, denuded for winter already, and noted that everything everywhere was brown, except for the scattered snow piles and patches of ice.

The wind, ever present in Casper, was worse than usual, nearly skittering the car into the oncoming lane as they headed east on 15th and then north on Kingsbury toward Casper Mountain. On auto pilot, Mimi corrected the minor skid; such moves are second nature when one grows up in Wyoming and cuts her driving teeth on black ice and whiteouts. She thought about what the sage old timers said about Casper's wind: *It will drive you crazy— really bat shit crazy. Why do you think we have one of the highest suicide rates in the country? It's the goddamned wind! Make you want to take yourself out, if not the whole town with you, sure enough! Nasty, damn, howlin' wind!*

If only it had been just the wind with Mike, Mimi thought. Just the wind and not a world of hurt. Somehow it would be easier to take. Man vs. Nature. Man loses. More base, more acceptable, more a freak-of-the-elements-eating-up-a man's-soul kind of disaster. But that would just be wishful thinking – wishful thinking and ostrich-headed denial of the true circumstances.

Mimi gave herself a bit of a shake, trying to push away these thoughts and focus on the task at hand. Then she dared to take her eyes off the slick street for a moment to look at Barby.

"Thanks for coming. I mean really thanks. I couldn't go over there alone, let alone tackle the clean up by myself or handle what I might find."

"And I wouldn't dream of letting you go by yourself. We'll just knuckle down, and we'll manage. We'll just manage," Barby said, determined. If she had reservations, she was doing a good job of concealing them.

"Well, you're a hell of a friend."

"You'd do the same for me. You'd surprise yourself," Barby said.

Mimi smiled a little, pleased that Barby thought she was capable of such selflessness. She wasn't so sure herself, but it was nice to know.

The two rode on mostly in silence other than attempting brief snippets of conversation, which went nowhere. They'd talked non-stop into the wee hours the night before, and they were now numb, exhausted, and talked out.

"OK. We're here," Mimi said at last after the twenty-minute drive that would have taken half that long without the ice. She pulled into the driveway of the new, two-story red-brick house that sat on a corner lot in a recently developed, moderately upscale neighborhood designed by Joe Mock, Mike's friend, just a few miles from the foot of the mountain. Because the house sat on a particularly windy corner, the snow had been blown off the driveway and into a tall drift against the back fence. "I hope this garage door opener works and that the inside door's not locked because she doesn't know where her house key is. She doesn't know where her head is, if you ask me." After she said that, she winced and looked quickly to see whether Barby had caught the unintended irony. She hadn't.

"Poor kid. I can't imagine," said Barby, with a slight shake of her head, focused on sorting out her own thoughts. "At least we can do this for her. It makes me feel good to *do something*, other than sit around and hold her hand and eat ham and hard rolls and tomato aspic and listen to well-meaning but misled people prattle on about how God never gives you more than you can handle. That, come to think of it, would be pretty ironic considering we're talking suicide here . . ."

"That's one of my all-time-favorite ludicrous, outrageous statements. As if a decent god—if there were one—would dangle despair over our heads just waiting to see how close he could get to making us crack. 'Let's see . . . one more calamity should do it . . . wouldn't want to overdo it . . . OOPS . . . there's a nervous breakdown, and, look, over here's a suicide . . . guess I went a bit too far this time . . . tee-hee.' What a ridiculous statement to make. It *was* good that you got *me* out of there as well, because if someone had had the temerity to say that, I think I might have decked 'em." Mimi hit the garage door button, holding her breath and sighing with relief as the door began to rise. And, as hoped, the door into the laundry room was not locked.

Her relief was, of course, short lived as the two made their way into the house. They both knew that what waited for them would probably crawl inside their heads and reappear during those low moments when thoughts turn ugly and pain is pervasive.

"So, you're sure the industrial-strength cleaning team has already been here, right?" Barby asked, just before they stepped into the kitchen. "So it shouldn't be all *that* bad?" The forced lilt in her voice made Mimi think of a child seeking confirmation when there was none to give. *My old dog will get better, won't he? Well, won't he?*

They both stood still, stalling, and looking away from each other.

"That's what they told me," Mimi said, but sounded none too sure. "They came in and sucked most of the blood out of the carpet. I just want to be sure they didn't miss anything before she comes back here. We are going to have to go over the place with a fine-toothed comb. Papa said that in twenty years of real estate dealings, he's heard of a couple of cases like this where they thought they'd cleaned up OK, but they'd missed things. A shotgun blast to the head is not a pretty thing."

At first glance, things looked normal: Cheerful yellow kitchen. Gingham curtains. Stair-stepped canisters. A bowl of pumpkin seeds soaking in salt water sitting next to the jack-o-lantern that Mike had carved the night before he checked out. Pleasant, homey space. Nothing out of place, and the floor looked recently scrubbed.

The two, cautious and slow, moved around the kitchen table and into the adjacent family room with Mimi in the lead. She stopped abruptly, causing Barby to nudge into her. Lying before them was the light-rust-colored carpet, clearly marked by a gruesome dark stain, the rust hue no match for the darkened blood-colored evidence of the shotgun blast to the head. No amount of cleaning could mitigate a stain like that.

Mimi spoke first. "What the hell. Well, clearly the carpet's got to go. She absolutely can't come back here to this. Bloody hell. Honest to god, literally bloody fucking hell."

"And look at the walls. There's fine spatter on them," Barby said as she edged around the room and peered closely. "Look at this wooden church mosaic—there are tiny drops on it. You don't see them at first, but they're there. I can try to clean it up, but I don't know if it will come out of this unpainted wood. Do we tell her? Do we just get rid of it?"

"No. We don't tell her. And we don't get rid of it. She's going to have to come to terms with some realities. We just do our best to soften . . . take the sharpest edge off. And then we have someone rip this disgusting carpet out and burn it. And we have professionals come in to paint.

Let's just move through these two rooms like detectives. Find every trace that the first crew missed. Jesus H. Look— right away I find something in plain sight."

Barby moved over to the sliding glass door where Mimi stood looking down at the rail on the left where the door would slide. They stared at a pea-sized, jagged-edged bone fragment, covered in dried blood and tissue.

Mimi paused, brought up short by the reality the fragment called into sharp focus. She stood staring at the glass door, which was still muddied from what she knew was Buddy's frantic scratching a few days earlier. He was now safely on Spruce Street, but he must be bewildered and distressed, as he had been home at the time of the gunshot and just on the other side of the sliding glass door.

Despite the wind, ice, and heartache, the sun shining cheerfully into the room sullied by violent death seemed cruel and anachronistic to Mimi. She stared at the dust floating in the warm beam filtering through the paw prints. *Must I hold a candle to my shames?* Mama's twenty-three years of teaching the *Merchant of Venice* had etched certain passages into her thinking, and the phrases geysered up randomly and frequently, only occasionally apropos.

Suddenly angry, she shook herself out of her short-lived trance and began to yank the cord to pull the heavy rust drapes across the face of the sun to block it out and to cover what she'd seen in the rail crevice. She'd deal with that later.

Barby stopped her, her touch gentle. "We'll need the light. You go fill the bucket with hot, soapy water, and I'll start picking up the bone fragments down there. Then we can scrub it better."

Mimi, wordless, obeyed. She was shocked that the professionals hadn't done a more thorough job. Papa had been right.

The two moved methodically around each of the rooms, scrutinizing every square inch. After a time monotony and tedium set in, and Barby attempted to lighten the moment.

"I know. Let's make this a contest. Whoever finds the biggest fragment, wins."

Mimi offered the hint of a smile, but it didn't form. Couldn't really form. But maybe sardonic humor would be preferable to the grim foreboding that had cast its spell up until now. *Whatever will get us through . . .*

Barby, as it turned out, won—lost, really. She had assigned herself the kitchen and was picking up and checking behind every item on the counters, even though they were twenty feet from where Mike had blown his brains out.

"Oh shit," she said. "Come and look at this."

Mimi came over and Barby pointed to a spot where the cookie jar had moments earlier concealed a chunk. A half-inch chunk of skull. Neat as a sugar cube, sitting like it belonged on the counter, right next to the salt.

Neither woman spoke. Barby gingerly picked up the piece with her Playtex-gloved hand and deposited it into the trash bag with the growing number of finer fragments of bone and small blobs of brain matter, all swaddled in paper towels.

But Mimi had her moment of—what? triumph?— when she, too, found a surprise. She'd noticed that there was a good two-inch gap under the door that led from the kitchen to the basement steps. *Bet the cleaning crew didn't think to open that door,* she thought. Sure enough, when she opened it, she immediately found a mass of brain matter on the first step. She felt lightheaded. She silently nudged Barby to look, and Barby turned away after taking a quick glance. She'd let Mimi handle that one and handle it Mimi did. More paper towels. More Mr. Clean. *Mr. Clean's bald head for Mike's splattered one.*

Barby, quiet again, moved on to a PVC-pipe-and-vinyl magazine rack that sat next to the recliner. Much to her horror, she realized that it was full of children's books, and upon closer observation, she discovered that a fine blood spatter covered them like a misting of spray paint.

"Holy shit. Now what do I do? Look, Mimi, the baby books are covered in blood."

Mimi squelched a gag. "We're book people. Normal people would just throw them away, but some of those have been in the family for generations. Can they be salvaged?"

"Well, they are mostly board books, it looks like. I think I can wipe them down. Is it worth trying?" Barby asked, clearly doubtful.

"I can't do it. You please try."

"I understand. Let me see what I can do." And she began with purpose to extricate each book from the pile to wipe it down, top to bottom and on the exposed sides. Neither said anything for a while. Then Barby came upon a small olive-green copy of *A Friend Is Someone Who Likes You* by Joan Walsh Anglund, a classic published in 1958.

Barby began to read aloud, her voice up an octave: "A friend is someone who likes you. A tree can be a friend. It gives you apples. The wind can be a friend. It sings soft songs to you . . ." At this juncture Barby interjected in her normal voice, "Not in Wyoming, where it'll beat the shit out of you."

Then she continued in falsetto, "A brook can be a friend. It talks to you with splashy gurgles . . ." Then she paused to make sure she'd caught Mimi's full attention before adding, "And a friend can be someone who helps you mop up a twelve-gauge suicide!" She then slammed the book closed and returned to her task, wiping down the book's cover, not looking at Mimi – who began to howl. Howled away the past three days of shock, anger, disbelief, grief, horror, and terror. Howled away the fear and the hatred and the rage. Howled and cried and howled some more.

Barby wasn't sure whether Mimi was laughing or crying or both, and she wasn't sure whether she should intercede. She stood back and let Mimi wind down, which took several minutes.

"Are you OK?" she finally managed after a moment of silence.

"Better," Mimi said. They both took a deep breath and carried on.

Second Place—*Card Sound Road*
Jacqueline Hope Derby—Louisville, Kentucky

The boy would not be ours. I entered the hospital's "Quiet Room" knowing immediately that the adoption had failed and our hope for another one slim. We'd poured everything we had into this one.

Looking around the room, I searched for the first boy I ever loved. Did he come unbidden in that moment to sit silent as a ghost beside me? Did tears stream down his face? Did he hold my hand? Did he put his arm around my husband and whisper, "I love you both," as we sat too stunned to grieve?

Where was my father in the hour of my heart's death?

I always take Card Sound Road from Florida City—the last failed tourist-trap mark on Florida's mainland—into the Keys. Sure, US-1 stretches more directly due-south, but my father cannot be found that way. His spirit lives in the mangrove marshes I drive by on the long stretch of the road, and I smell his Aramis mingling in the piquant salty air. I hear his double-outboard motors reverse as he expertly brings his boat alongside the dock at Alabama Jack's—an open-air dive bar lined with Harleys outside that reeks of fried seafood—the only stop out here. He greets me as I give the toll-booth guy my dollar before heading over the bridge. I see him in the whole of the sky and sea as we top the bridge, and my eyes quickly dart between the road and Barnes Sound. My father has retired his spirit to the Florida Keys, just as it was always there when he was living.

My first memory of Card Sound Road is sitting between my parents in an impossibly long line of traffic attempting to cross the bridge after a holiday weekend. Maybe this is why I always think of Daddy when I come this way. With our boat, *Popcorn*, trailing behind us, we'd move in inches north up US-1 toward the turn-off toward Card Sound Road. Daddy pointed out to me eagles' nests atop different light posts as we went.

We'd spent the weekend at America Outdoors Camper Resort, a Key Largo campground and dock we frequented. I can still taste in my mouth the Firecracker popsicles my friend Kelly and I always bought in their convenience store and can still feel the grit of sand in my battered flip-flops as we stood in the hot sun in our bikinis licking and slurping furiously. I look for its old abandoned sign in the thicket as I pass where it once was, but it has succumbed to time and new developments.

Daddy is in Key Largo but not the way he's in Islamorada. Other than America Outdoors, all of my memories of Key Largo are from after he died. Key lime pie at Mrs. Mac's Kitchen with my friend Matt, or dinner with my mother and her third husband at Sundowner's. Daddy is not there. I once took a class to learn how to ocean kayak at Florida Bay Outfitters, and Matty and I would go on kayaking tours with one of their guides through those blessed mangroves with nurse sharks darting below us. My father would whistle through the mangroves like he always does, but his spirit does not live there.

You first have to get through Tavernier and the Tavernier Creek Marina where *Popcorn* was in dry dock a while. Many of the drawbridges on the Overseas Highway are gone now, but I still remember waiting for them with him here. We'd stop at the Winn-Dixie on the way further south, so when I see it pass me on the right a memory dings as a distant bell. What did we buy? Where were we going? I don't remember. What I know is that in Tavernier, the urge to run to him almost overwhelms me. I'm giddy with anticipation.

I then put Windley Key in my review mirror. The tourist traps with their hundred-dollar conch shells, overbaked white people, and cheap ads for even cheaper bathing suits fade too. We will be together again soon.

It is here in the archipelago between Islamorada and Marathon that he resides. I pick him up in Upper Matecumbe Key, and he points out to me things that have changed since we were last here together over forty years ago. He tells me about his recent rare steak at Cheeca Lodge, and how he loves taking their guests out to do flat-bottom fishing. He stands on their pier and watches the sun rise over the Atlantic each morning. *Jacqueline, can you smell the light here? It is clean and bright and fills your lungs with life everlasting.*

We always stop at Anne's Beach in Lower Matecumbe Key, like we did the beautiful clear-blue afternoon exactly one week after the baby who would not be ours was born. Through astral projection, I once spent a day with him at this three-strip meeting of road, mangrove, water. First, we waded in the water on the long, winding, submerged sandbar on which you can walk far out into the ocean, watching the tide come in around us as blue crabs scurry away from our feet. The fin of a blue marlin appeared in the distance as it looked for an early morning breakfast. The herons fed close to shore, painstakingly picking up their feet as they too stalked their prey. We stood together in the water just watching—at one with each other, the water, the sky. A feather floated to me on the slightest wave as a peace offering from him. He knows I'm still pissed that he up and died. Six is too young to lose your father.

We then climbed into his boat and zoomed over the chop to go fishing for snapper. We always fished for snapper on *Popcorn*. We wrestle our reels and rods, and he cleans all the fish for me just like when I was small and catching bait off Dinner Key. We drink ice-cold Cokes or root beers or bourbons on the rocks. The sun melts us by the end of day, but when the time comes to turn toward the blazing streaks of purple, magenta, and awe we feel invigorated again. A pod of dolphins leaps with joy beside us as we head back toward the shore now visible only as dots of green palms, waterfront homes, and white streaks of bridges in the distance. Daddy still wears his black Wayfarers with the green lenses, and he steers us with the relaxed confidence he always wore in real life.

He glances over at me quickly to get my attention. *Do you feel God right now?*

Yes. I do. I look at him hard and long and in a new adult light. *What do you believe about God, Daddy?*

I never really found God in a building or a religion— not like your mother did. God is here. See those dolphins, sweetheart? They are God to me. This sky. This is God to me. This water. That sunset. All God.

Me too Daddy. I find God here. Every time.

After my husband and I stopped at Anne's Beach the week after were turned away from adopting the boy we would've named Schuyler, we travelled to Key West to find each other in the storm of our grief. We slept late each day, only waking to watch the Property Brothers as the parking lot of the motel flooded in the early May rains. We'd venture out for a quick lunch, and then tumble back into bed, pulling the white, slightly salty and damp sheets around us. At night, we'd eat amazing food, get drunk, make love or fuck, and then weep once again for a future imagined but never to be lived. Around my ring finger, next to my old wedding ring, was a tiny silver band with "SCHUYLER" stamped in simple block lettering. It burned hotter each day.

On the way back to Miami, we stopped in yet another downpour at the Island Fish Company in Marathon for lunch. On the wall hung a massive photo of a fishing contest from the mid-thirties. There in the faces of young fresh boys was my father beaming back at me. He must have been seventeen in the photograph.

There you are, I whispered to him with my hand on his face in vintage black-and-white.

After lunch, we ran back to our car, and Daddy tucked in beside us for our desperate-for-a-grave-site-but-none-to-be-found ritual at our precious Anne's Beach.

We found it nearly flooded when we arrived. Alone in the parking lot, my husband took the ring from me and stood in the deluge wading as close to the water's edge as he could and with all the strength of a broken heart hurled the ring into the water where my father caught it and carried it out to sea and out to whatever real God might exist.

I heard him again whisper. This sky. This water. You, daughter.

My husband folds himself wet and trembling back into the car. Tears and rain undiscernibly mix. I don't want to cry any more for my dead—my dead father or dead dream of motherhood or dead faith in anything other than the blessed South Florida sky. I gingerly pull back onto US-1 and head north in the blinding rain. The red and white of the Circle K at the fork in northern Key Largo calls to me like the heartbeat sound a bird must discern to head home again. I trace in my mind the inevitable veer to the right toward Card Sound Road where I will start grieving as I leave my father behind once again.

Third Place—*The Coming of Karalyn*
DJ Buchanon—Tallahassee, Florida

My heart thrilled as I ended the phone call from the Department of Children and Families.

My husband James and I had just been invited to a discussion about a little eight-year-old girl who might become our adopted daughter! At the conference we would learn enough about her to decide whether we wanted to move to the next step. The girl's long-term psychologist and our DCF caseworker, Sharon Lawrence, would meet with us.

We had begun the process of adopting a child from Florida's foster care system two years earlier. Following an initial training course we were assigned to Sharon's caseload. She shepherded us through the next seven months of interviews, paperwork, and home studies, and once we were approved to adopt, she inaugurated the hunt for our perfect match.

After much soul-searching, James and I had concluded that our strengths and capabilities would probably mesh well with the needs of a little girl who had suffered any type of abuse or neglect. Waiting while we sought our match was tough. I wanted to start making a positive difference in a child's life without delay! I found myself daydreaming all the time, picturing myself loving a child who needed me. From time to time, Sharon told us about this girl or that one, but usually another couple was in line before us, or some other impediment arose. So, months and months passed in futile search.

Now we showed up at the appointed time. After introductions, Sharon disclosed that Karalyn, the little girl, was a victim in a terrible abuse case. Karalyn had four older brothers, and during her early years there were numerous abuse investigations at the home where they lived with their mother and stepfather. Unfortunately, Child Protective Services was unable to glean sufficient evidence to make a case.

I listened in dismay as Sharon went on. "Then, when Karalyn was five, her stepfather hanged her and one of the boys from a tree by their ankles, and the mother did absolutely nothing about it. Finally, CPS was able to take immediate action to file charges and arrest both adults."

Linda Clevinger, the psychologist, picked up the tale. "It took almost three years for the criminal case to be resolved, and meanwhile Karalyn was separated from her brothers and placed in one foster home after another. Her psychological problems, which include PTSD and bed-wetting, were so severe that the foster parents were overwhelmed by the amount of time it took to see to her needs. They couldn't take care of her *and* the other foster kids in their homes. So, Karalyn was passed from place to place."

Linda paused, and what followed was much more upbeat, "Nevertheless, I think Karalyn has a lot of potential that could be developed in the right environment! She's smart, she's usually cheerful, and she tries to do right. Plus she has a great sense of humor!"

Sharon took over again. "Karalyn's mother and stepfather went to court last April, and they will spend a long time in prison for what they did to their kids. The court also severed all parental rights, so all five kids became available for adoption.

"But then, something went wrong. The boys were placed quickly, and Karalyn went to a nice couple in Bristol, fifty miles west of here. They still hope to adopt Karalyn, but their caseworker made a mistake. They aren't eligible to foster or adopt because they're cohabiting, not married. Unfortunately the error wasn't discovered until Karalyn was already living with them. Anyway, no one has yet informed them that Karalyn cannot stay with them."

The story and the sadness of the current situation left James and me subdued, but we recovered enough to ask questions and receive candid answers. With only a glance between us we agreed that we were still very interested in taking the next step toward the adoption of Karalyn. Final decisions would come later, but arrangements could now be made to meet Karalyn.

The work done by DCF is a messy business. Its representatives must dig into complicated family situations and do the best they can for their clients. Sharon Lawrence was now compelled to deal with the unsanctioned placement of Karalyn with Rhonda and Joe, the couple Karalyn was living with. Until James and I entered the equation Sharon had left well enough alone, but now there was no choice. Because of the sensitive situation, Sharon would oversee the entire process of transferring Karalyn into our home.

Our hearts went out to all of them. I do not like the way things happened. It was a grim business, but Karalyn would have eventually been taken from Rhonda and Joe anyway. I didn't feel guilt, only sadness and sympathy.

Three days after our conference, Sharon informed us that she would visit Rhonda and Joe that night, and give the bad news to them. She intended to allow Karalyn to remain in their household while Karalyn became acquainted with James and myself, and acclimated to the idea of the change.

Though Karalyn might pay us a visit to see our house, it would be a month or so before she made the final transfer.

We were fine with that. We wanted to do this right, with as little turmoil for Karalyn as possible. We were prepared for the inconvenience of traveling the hundred miles every weekend so that we three could get to know one another. Besides, our house was not ready. Karalyn's soon-to-be bedroom was full of miscellaneous stuff piled all over. We needed the time to set up a bedchamber suitable for a little girl.

James and I spent a solemn, pensive evening. We held a sort of vigil, our own excitement and anticipation being tempered by mindfulness of the heartbreak occurring in Bristol. We sorrowed over the fact that bringing Karalyn into our home would necessarily cause her even more trauma, initially. There was nothing we could do to mitigate anyone's pain. At about eleven that evening, we finally went to bed, figuring that, by then, the worst was over for Karalyn, Rhonda, and Joe.

The next morning at work I expected a call from Sharon to tell me how the evening went. My phone rang less than an hour after I got to my office. It was Sharon, all right, but tension was thick in her voice.

She got right to the point. "I hate to do this to you like this, Jeanne, but can you take Karalyn today?"

Taken aback, I stammered, "You mean to see the house? For a visit?"

"No, for good! Rhonda says she and Karalyn cried all night. Everyone is distraught. Rhonda says it's too heartbreaking, and she doesn't want to stretch things out. She wants Karalyn to go now, and get it over with!"

I managed to gasp out, "Yes, of course, we'll take her! If Rhonda's sending Karalyn away, we certainly don't want her to go anywhere else!"

Sharon promised to call my home number later to set a rendezvous.

Well! So much for our plans for a gentle get-acquainted period! With shaky hands, I sent a cryptic text to James, asking him to meet me at home. Then I grabbed my purse and hastily arranged with my boss to take the rest of the week off. I already had leave time approved for this purpose, but no one expected I would need it so soon, or on such short notice.

At home, James met me at the door with a look of puzzlement. "I got your message. What's happening?"

Rushing past him, I told him over my shoulder, "Well, things are going crazy, and we're going to bring Karalyn home tonight, for good! We've got to get ready!"

So, we spent a couple of hours hastily shifting things out of what was to be Karalyn's bedroom, heaping stuff haphazardly onto the furnishings in another room for the time being, all the while discussing the new developments. After I vacuumed and dusted Karalyn's empty room, I surveyed it with some dismay. No furniture; the walls were scuffed and scraped, and the carpet had stains.

The room was shabby, not our best; I wished it was more attractive. Yet, despite its present condition, this was on purpose. The room awaited a little girl who could participate in fixing up the room when she was ready to express her own preferences. At least it was clean now, and the sun beamed through the large window, which was a saving grace.

We made up an air mattress on the floor to suffice until we could buy some nice furniture for her room. Just as we were finishing up, Sharon called to tell us how and when to get to the transfer location. Because of the distance, we had to leave right away.

So, after years of preparation and waiting, the time arrived at last for us to meet our new daughter.

Joe and Rhonda chose to bring Karalyn to a McDonald's restaurant just outside of Bristol. They would surrender her there, in neutral territory, instead of at their house. James and I met up with Sharon in the parking lot and she led us through the rearmost door of the McDonald's dining area, where three people were sitting just inside. I didn't know what to expect, and feared a tearful scene. Sharon made the introductions; there was Rhonda, whose inner tumult was evident, but controlled. The man was Joe, who lived with Rhonda and shared household responsibilities. Of course, the little girl with the ice cream treat was Karalyn. We all worked to establish and maintain a civil atmosphere.

Karalyn's thick strawberry-blonde hair was cut in a bob that made her head resemble a pumpkin. The sides hugged her cheeks and curved under her chin. Her bangs reached just below her eyebrows. The result was an aperture about four inches wide on the front of her head, from which she peered from time to time. She mostly kept her head down, which put her whole face in shadow. Surprisingly, she seemed to be in good control of herself too, apparently torn between her grief and curiosity.

As if hoping to make us reject her, Karalyn raised her head and advised us in a soft voice that she had a bed-wetting problem. She regarded us with interest, to see how we would react to the information. I assured her we knew about it, and that we could help her. She settled back again.

Sharon controlled the encounter, so except when spoken to, I frankly gaped and drank in the sight of Karalyn. After Karalyn's one comment about bedwetting, she did not speak anymore. However, there was a moment when she peeked with one coy green eye around the curtains of her hair, and we locked gazes. I couldn't help but smile at her, and I was astonished when she dimpled and a small return smile appeared at her mouth. Then she sort of shrugged, dipped her head, and hid under her hair again. My chest swelled in admiration for her courage. Where did she get the fortitude to smile in what had to be a devastating situation for her?

At the same time, I felt terrible for Rhonda and Joe, who were behaving heroically. During the four months that Karalyn lived with them, Rhonda had lavished Karalyn with care and opened her heart to her. Rhonda bestowed Karalyn with a pink and silver bicycle and several other minor treasures. I believe Rhonda was capable of being a wonderful mother. Now, Karalyn would be torn from her, and there was nothing to be done about it. DCF would have its way.

The air crackled with tension, and Sharon kept things as brief as was decent. While Karalyn, Rhonda, and Joe made their final good-byes, James and I put Karalyn's overnight bag into our car. We would come back in a day or so to collect the remainder of her possessions.

Without further delay, Sharon ended the meeting and scooped a tear-streaked but resigned Karalyn away and into her own car. Karalyn would ride with her to our house while James and I drove by ourselves, leading the way.

The sun was low as we drove home, shining upon a line of storm clouds towering in front of us. A large rainbow sprang into existence, exquisite and complete. It shone for several minutes, lovely, feeling like an omen of good things to come. I hoped Karalyn saw it too, and that she took it for a good sign.

When we arrived back home that evening, Linda Clevinger, Karalyn's psychologist whom we had previously met, was waiting there, having been summoned by Sharon to help ease Karalyn into her new home. Karalyn had known Linda for a long time and was comfortable with her. They talked quietly in the family room.

I was itching to get more acquainted with Karalyn, but James and I were busy with Sharon. There were endless forms to sign, custody papers and documents entitling us to act on Karalyn's behalf (within legal parameters), and so on. Karalyn was still a ward of the state for now, so our rights would be limited until the adoption was final.

When the paperwork was complete, Sharon handed us a heavy stack of psychological reports and other previously confidential information about Karalyn. It felt surreal to receive them now. Everything known about Karalyn was in those pages. If we had been able to move into this situation slowly, as planned, we would have read all this stuff and made an informed decision about taking Karalyn in. Now it was too late for that, and our decision was made anyway. Our Karalyn was with us, and would stay!

Sharon and Linda prepared to leave. The long, long wait, the anticipation, and the frantic arrangements of the day were over. Now, two hours after first setting eyes on her, James and I would be left on our own with the little girl who was to be our daughter. Despite all the waiting, all the training, everything we had gone through, I suddenly panicked.

"What do we do now?" I asked Linda desperately. "What if there's a problem?"

She smiled. "You just live your lives. Do what you do every day, and deal with whatever comes up. You have what it takes to handle just about anything that's likely to happen. Anyway, you have my number in case you truly need backup. Assuming all goes well, I'll see you at Karalyn's regular appointment week after next." Then, giving Karalyn a final hug of support, Linda made her exit.

Short Story
Final Judge—Saundra Kelley
Tallahassee, Florida

First Place—Canal Cat
Brett Herrmann—Spring Valley, Illinois

All you could see was the head trying to stay above water. Just a speck of the cat's white fur stuck out of the murky water as it inched closer and closer to the shore.

"What was that?" asked a fisherman on the shore, looking up to the bridge above him.

A handful of people had their lines cast in the water at the Illinois and Michigan Canal in La Salle, Ill. before the bag was tossed from the highway overhead. The former shipping canal now acted as a popular recreation spot, even drawing the more dedicated anglers to fish on the mild mid-November day. But no one was expecting to catch a kitten.

The little swimmer wasn't even to shore when a young boy who was there with his mother scooped it up in a fishing net. The kitten was set down on the tow path as people gathered around it. It whined out high pitched "meows" as it shivered. The cat's white fur was matted down against its frail body. It was tiny, like someone stuck chicken bones in a wet wool sock. A small black spot on its forehead was its only identifying mark.

"Where are the rest?" asked one of the fishermen.

"The rest?" asked the boy's mother.

"It was a whole bag that was dumped from the bridge," the fishermen said. "There were more."

The young boy spotted a purple canvas tote bag floating in the water. He cast his line, hooked the bag, and reeled it in.

It was empty.

"Who would do this?" the mother said.

Alex felt the last bump as the truck turned off of the asphalt road and into the gravel driveway. He lay flat on his stomach in the bed of the truck, his head buried in his arms. Dad told him to keep low so police did not see him, but he didn't feel like showing his face to anyone after what just happened. Dad killed the engine and Alex heard the driver's side door open and close. But Alex kept his head down. As he tried to fight back tears his face burned hot despite the cool fall air.

"Come on, buddy, you can get up now," Dad said.

Alex didn't budge.

"Hey, I know it's tough. But this was what we had to do. We couldn't keep all of them," Dad said. "One's enough."

About an hour earlier in the day, Alex had never been so excited to see Dad's face. Now, he couldn't bring himself to look at him. Alex was one day away from Thanksgiving break in his first year at Northwest Elementary School—fourth grade. Dad moved him to La Salle earlier in the year to be closer to Grandma. Grandma needed to watch Alex often because Dad had a career as a lineworker, maintaining power lines wherever he was needed. That meant a lot of local work, but anytime a natural disaster wreaked havoc, Dad was on the road. That's why Alex was so excited to see him when he got off the school bus.

Dad had been gone for about five weeks working in the city of Washington, Ill., which had been devastated by a tornado outbreak. Alex had not seen much of his father since starting school, which left him without the one person he felt he could talk to. He was shy at school. He wasn't ever picked on, but he had a hard time making friends and spent most recesses wandering around the playground by himself. His teacher, Ms. Harris, had intervened a few times to get him into games of kickball or freeze tag, but Alex was more interested in observing bugs or squirrels than he was in sports. Those interests went unshared with his classmates. About the only person he confided in was Dad. And other than dad, the only other creature he confided in was his cat, Peanuts.

Peanuts was a stray they found the day they were moving in with Grandma in La Salle—about a week after mom left for good. Alex was standing in his new room eating a PayDay candy bar. The room was empty save for a twin mattress sitting on the brown carpet. Sunlight cut through the open window before Peanuts started walking across the sill, his shadow growing large on the bedroom floor. The cat stopped and stared at Alex, who slowly approached the window, offering a piece of his candy bar. Peanuts hopped inside and devoured the salty treat. She had been in and out of Alex's room ever since.

At first, Dad thought the cat was Grandma's. But Grandma insisted she never had a cat. Grandma was also in the early stages of Alzheimer's disease, so Dad didn't always take what she said as a fact. Alex took care of her as much as she took care of him. But she could still cook and drive as needed when Dad was out of the house, which had turned out to be more often than expected. So, when Dad was on the road, Peanuts (named after her favorite candy bar) became Alex's confidante. But like the kids at school, Peanuts didn't like being too close to Alex. He would try and hold her and she would break out the claws, resulting in a few scratches. But every morning he would wake up with Peanut's curled up at the foot of his mattress even though she had not been there before he went to bed.

Alex had always thought the cat was a boy up until recently. He noticed the cat putting on weight (Alex thought it might have been too many PayDay's) but that was all explained shortly after Dad left for tornado duty. Alex came home from school one day to find four new kittens on his bedroom floor. And for the next few weeks, his friend circle grew that much bigger. He spent hours laying on his floor, writing in his notebook how the kittens developed day after day. He found an old cardboard toaster box in the house and lined it with towels. He placed the cats inside while Peanuts kept a close eye, never straying far from the box. The first kitten Alex named was Spot, due to the little black patch of fur on its forehead that stuck out from the rest of its white fur. The other kittens were grey, and Alex named them Daisy, Smokey and Clint.

When Dad did return home, one of the first thing he asked when Alex shared the news about the kittens was if they had names.

"That's only going to make this harder," Dad said.

The school bus had just dropped Alex off at his stop when he saw Dad waiting for him for the first time in weeks. Alex sprinted off the school bus to hug him before they started walking home. Alex ran ahead to the front door to go get the box of kittens in his room. By this time they had started to walk, but could still be found sleeping in the cardboard box most of the time. Dad's face scrunched in displeasure when he saw Alex emerge from his room with the kittens.

"That damn cat isn't fixed?" he said. "Ma, you have to get the cat spayed."

"It's not my cat," she said from her recliner. She was fixated on Jeopardy! on the television.

"We can't keep the kittens, Alex. I'm not having a house full of cats around here.

Grandma already has enough on her plate taking care of you when I'm not here." Dad said.

"But I've been taking good care of them," Alex said.

"Well, I'm not paying for vet expenses on five cats now. I wasn't expecting to pay for one," Dad said. "But I know the cat . . ."

"Peanuts," Alex interrupted.

". . . Yes, Peanuts, has been important to you," Dad said. "But the rest have to go."

"Go where?" Alex asked.

"Go. Go . . ." Dad trailed off. "Growing up when we had the farm property, the barn cats seemed to have another litter about every week, so we would put them in a burlap sack with some bricks and throw them in the creek," Dad said.

"You'd get about twenty or thirty of them running around if you didn't," Grandma added, her eyes still glued to the TV.

"I'm going to find a bag. You go hop in the back of the truck with the litter," Dad said.

He couldn't do it on the first pass through. The meowing from the back was faint, especially with the wind roaring around him in the open truck bed. His arms seemed frozen in place as they cleared the bridge span.

Dad opened the back window and shouted back to him.

"Come on, buddy. This needs to be done. It's your cat and it's your responsibility," he said.

Alex started shaking uncontrollably. He wasn't sure if it was from the cool air or his nerves but he couldn't stop. The truck slowed down as Dad found an opening to pull a U-turn. They were making their second approach at the bridge and Alex shut his eyes hard. He heard the rolling of the tires switch from asphalt to the higher pitched, hollow noise of the bridge concrete. He swung the bag high into the air, losing his balance slightly. Then he crumpled. He lay lifeless in the bed until they were back home. And he continued to sit motionless until Dad picked him up and brought him inside, placing him on the couch. Even then, Alex couldn't look up. He wasn't crying anymore. But he knew that if he looked at his Dad the waterworks would start right back up. He'd waited so many days to tell him about the kittens. Now they were gone.

"I know that was hard for you, but I'm proud of you," Dad said. "It feels bad now, but you'll get over it. Just takes a little time."

Alex buried his head further into the couch cushions.

"Tell you what. Tomorrow is your last day before Thanksgiving break right? I'll pick you up after school and we can hang out and play video games all night. I'm sure you've been practicing Mario Kart," Dad said. Alex still did not move.

"And then first thing Wednesday morning, we'll get on out to Tanner's Orchard." he said.

Finally, Alex's head popped up. Tanner's Orchard had been a tradition for their family every fall. But since Mom was gone and Dad was working all of the time, Alex didn't think they would be going this year. They usually did around Halloween, but they were well past that holiday. For the first time in almost an hour, Alex looked at Dad's face and he was able to hold back tears.

"Can we get apple cider donuts?" Alex said.

"Anything you want," Dad said.

Alex usually hated show and tell. His old school never had it, so it wasn't until this year that he realized how much he loathed it. It required public speaking, a big fear of his. But Ms. Harris had made it a point to keep it going each month. Alex had brought in Peanuts once and he was hoping to bring in her kittens this time before yesterday's incident. However, he did have a good backup plan. Dad let him bring in his work hardhat, which had a lot of different stickers Dad explained to him the night before. He had spent about an hour before bed rattling off everything his dad had told him in his head before finally falling asleep.

"Cool hat," said Janie, who sat to Alex's left.

"Thanks. It's my dad's," Alex said.

Janie was one of the few classmates who tried to talk to Alex. She was popular with just about everyone. The anticipation to tell her about the hardhat—to tell everyone—had him bouncing his leg underneath his desk.

But going in alphabetical order, he was second in the class to speak. First was Adam, who bolted up when Ms. Harris gave him an introduction.

"Adam has a very interesting story for us today," she said. "Go ahead when you're ready."

Adam had printed out a picture taken of him holding a white kitten with a little black spot on its forehead. The young boy launched into his story.

"Yesterday, my mom took me fishing at the canal after school . . ."

Alex couldn't focus on the words being spoken. He fixated on the picture of the wet kitten in Adam's arms. It felt like a hot ball of lead was moving through his intestines.

"Spot," he said under his breath. *"Spot."*

". . . now the kitten is at the rescue shelter getting his shots. They said we could pick him up this afternoon. We're going to name him Survivor," Adam said.

"Thank you, Adam. That's great your family is going to be able to rescue the kitten. It's really awful that someone would do something like this. I hope no one here thinks it's OK to do something like that to another living creature," Ms. Harris said.

"Yeah, the police said they would be looking for who did it," Adam said.

"Well, maybe we will see some justice," Ms. Harris said. She turned and looked at Alex. So did Janie. So did the rest of the class.

"Alex, what have you brought for us today?" she asked.

Every muscle in Alex's body was petrified, except for his lips, which trembled uncontrollably. The more he tried to look calm, the worse it got. Ms. Harris noticed the anguish in his face.

"Is everything alright?" she asked.

Alex could barely manage to croak out the words without sobbing.

"I don't feel good," was all he could manage before the tears started.

"Okay, it's alright. Why don't you come outside with me?" she said. "Brittany, get ready to go next."

Alex stood up from his desk with his hands wiping tears away from his face. Every eye in the classroom was looking at him. A couple of boys in the back started giggling as he made it to the door with Ms. Harris right behind him. They stepped into the hallway and Ms. Harris put a hand on his shoulder.

"What's wrong? Was it Adam's story? I know it might have been upsetting," she said.

Alex couldn't find any words. The hot ball of lead in his stomach had stopped moving, but now it was expanding.

"My stomach hurts," he said.

"OK. I can send you to the office. We'll have the nurse call your dad. We're about done for the day anyway," Ms. Harris said.

Dad. The thought of Dad just made the pain worse. But Alex thought leaving would be better than going back in the classroom. The school nurse let him sit on the couch while the office secretary contacted his home. The nurse questioned what his symptoms were, but he really couldn't offer anything other than what he told Ms. Harris.

"My stomach hurts," he said again and again.

Alex watched the clock move second by second as he waited for his dad to show up. Only a few minutes passed before the secretary walked in and said his ride had arrived. Alex slung his backpack over his shoulders and stepped outside, his dad's helmet in his hand.

It was not Dad's truck in the parking lot. It was Grandma's old Buick and the sight of it seemed to stop the swelling in the ball of lead in his stomach. He walked up to the car and opened the door to the back seat. Sitting in a ray of sunlight behind Grandma was Peanuts. Alex took off his backpack and got in the car, buckling his seatbelt, but not touching his pet cat. He knew Peanuts did not like it when he was too aggressive.

"School said you're feeling sick," Grandma said, keeping her eyes facing forward as the car lurched into drive. "Do you need to go to the hospital? Your dad got called back out to work again and I'll need to get the insurance information if we're going to the hospital."

Once the car started moving, Alex dropped his dad's hardhat on the floor. Peanuts stood up and stretched her back. Slowly, she walked across the bench seat before climbing right into Alex's lap. She nuzzled her head against his arm before closing her eyes. Then the purring started.

"I think I'm feeling better," Alex said. "I just want to go home."

Second Place—Balthazar's Love Travail
Crew Schielke—Bloomfield, New Jersey

I first learned how to sit in full-lotus by suffering slowly for a long time. For years, I'd believed that someone like me, a product of western culture, raised with people who sat on chairs, rather than crossed-legged on the floor, was simply incapable of achieving this position. There was also the very real possibility that I'd injure myself attempting to push the limits of my inflexibility.

At forty, the last thing I wanted was to tear a ligament or to otherwise hurt my knees stretching, losing precious training time for such a preposterous reason. I was already too old to hope to earn a black belt before my body started coaxing my mind to retire my gi for good. Every strained neck, pulled muscle, or outbreak of ring worm, caused grievous consternation. Not just over lost time, but on account of the irritability that came with being off the mats.

By gradually working one half-lotus at a time, with little baby steps, and counting my breaths like an aspiring yogi, I achieved full-lotus in less than a month of regular practice. What I found most surprising was how quickly my feeling of self-satisfaction faded, then disappeared altogether, only to be replaced by an unexpected sensation of physical balance while sitting, allowing me to enjoy the position until my knees ached, and I had to untangle myself.

Soon, I found myself sitting in full-lotus whenever possible, for as long as I could endure, with the idea that this would help increase my flexibility, thereby enabling me to perform more advanced Rubber Guard jujitsu

2019 Seven Hills Review

techniques. Patience was on my side. My ulterior motive was to enhance my fighting prowess. This made it easier to detach, relax and to follow my breath. I tried guiding energy up and down my spine, following what I half-remembered from a podcast on Kriya Yoga that I'd listened to in my car years earlier. Lifting laser-like attention up from the bottom of my spine to an imaginary flower sprouting at the crown of my head, I passively followed my breath for a long time, hours maybe.

I wasn't looking for a revelation and had no spiritual aspirations. Instead, I was just enjoying peacefulness, and elasticity of body and mind. Suddenly, at 6:47AM, on February 14, 2017, something incredible and unexpected happened.

There was a burst of light. It was first red, then yellow, and then purple and green, not white. I was falling. I opened my eyes and saw the time on the cable box. But I could not move or think, or even scream. Sensations of hot, then cold, followed by visions that flung me out of my room, and sent me flying low over huge expanses of wind driven water. Then high over massive forests of green trees, the sweet smell of sticky-pine convincing me that I was trapped inside a lucid dream.

I hiccupped . . . and was back on the floor in my room, shaking, or so it seemed. Yet, I could see that I was sitting perfectly still. After about twenty breaths, whatever had a hold of me let go, and I was free. My knees ached, and my underwear was drenched with sweat. There was a puddle on my yoga mat where I'd been sitting. I got up and walked down stairs right out the front door and stood in a daze on the porch, sucking in shallow breaths of fresh air through clenched teeth.

That morning, I had no appetite. I was distracted and unable to convince myself to go to work. Instead, I drove around listlessly, doing donuts in the snow in my Chevy Blazer SUV, trying to get over a sensation of morbid disquietude. As I was driving, my field of vision expanded unaccountably. My blind spot disappeared, and I could see everything around me, even with my eyes closed, like I was a Jedi using the force. Somehow this disturbed me more than I found it exhilarating.

My theory was that I had unleashed, quite accidentally, some ancient yogic power, causing a transformation of my psyche. Unfortunately, the transformation seemed incomplete. Perhaps I wasn't ready, or had interrupted the process while it was happening, out of fear and ignorance, or by hiccupping. Intense anxiety overwhelmed me, a vortex of distress swirled inside my chest. I began to feel drained and extremely ill-at-ease. It occurred to me that I may have irreparably damaged my nervous system, exacerbating some latent insanity. A Google search provided no enlightenment.

My slow-churning-panic did not subside; nor did it immediately grow worse. By noon, I decided to sit down again on my yoga mat to try to complete my metamorphosis.

Third Place—*The Steam*
Ashley Daugherty—Tallahassee, Florida

As the steam cleared from the last of the explosions they could see that the old record store was all that remained. To Harley this was sign. The record store had always been his home away from home. Now it was the only one he had left. He needed to go back to find his family if he could bring them here, but Harley stood motionless in the wake of a disaster. What to do? His body would not cooperate.

Harley stood frozen for what felt like an eternity but was only a few moments. Slowly his feet shuffled forward moving slowly towards the old record store Forever Vinyl. The sign hanging on for dear life. Harley approached the door, a small push and it opened. Forever Vinyl looked untouched inside. All the records organized by musical genre. All perfectly alphabetized. But where was Bruce the owner? Bruce had been like a second father to Harley he was sure he would let him and his family take shelter here, but he needed to ask first. Where is he? Harley wondered.

Harley approached the counter where Bruce always sat on his stool listening to bygone days forever recorded on vinyl. It was strange to see Bruce's stool turned over. Harley set it up straight. Apocalypse or not Bruce would want his seat and his tunes. "Har-Lee" a voice rasped in the back. "Issss . . . Thhaaat you?" Harley tensed but followed the sound of the voice behind the curtain to the back room. A stairwell led to the above apartment, once an office, that Bruce had turned into a tiny living space. Bruce was fond of saying he didn't need much as long as he had good tunes downstairs. That was what Harley loved about

Bruce. His minimalist nature and his love of music. He had taught Harley that.

Harley felt dread in his heart. There at the bottom of the stairwell laid Bruce, sprawled out on the floor both legs splayed and broken at odd sickening angles. "Harrley" Bruce wheezed. "I'm glad it's you son" he coughed up blood and spat. "When the explosion hit, I hightailed it down the stairs" said Bruce. "If I'm going to die in a fiery blaze, I want a good song to go out on, something righteous" said Bruce.

"Like Led Zeppelin?" asked Harley softly.

"That's my boy" Bruce wheezed. "I taught you well" said Bruce. "Put on some Skeeter Davis" said Bruce. No song could be more appropriate thought Harley. He didn't want to leave Bruce but a last wish from a dying man for a song was not something he could say no to.

Harley walked quickly through the curtain to Bruce's countertop. His record player was ready. He grabbed Skeeter from Bruce's stash and it began to play the end of the world. Harley held back tears as he moved back behind the curtain to sit with his dying friend. "All of this is yours now." Bruce whispered no longer wheezing. "I left it to you in my will, you're as good as the son I never had." said Bruce. Tears streamed down Harley's face so moving was the gift but what was Forever Vinyl without Bruce Wilson the heart and soul of the establishment? "Bruce," Harley whispered. "Please I . . . his voice trailed off. Bruce put his hand on Harley's arm. Looking up at him with Skeeter Davis singing the end of the world in the background he smiled and closed his eyes. "Take care of the records and enjoy the tunes son." said Bruce. "Music saves us all in the end, one way or another."

Bruce stopped breathing but died with a smile on his lips. Harley began to weep softly. The steam was evaporating outside, and the sun was coming through. Harley sat by his friend and cried. He would have to find his family soon if they we even alive. He would bring them here to Forever Vinyl, their new home. Harley would wait though he wanted to enjoy one last tune with his friend.

Flash Fiction

Final Judge— Anna Yeatts
Pinehurst, North Carolina

First Place—*Bear Waltz*
John Brantingham—Walnut, California

Don hears the shot before he feels it pass through his thigh, missing the bone but cutting through some meat and the femoral artery. He stumbles but keeps his feet. It seems important to stay upright, but he saw enough of the war to know that he's going to die. His first instinct is to yell at his son not to shoot blindly into a bush, but he realizes that the boy has a lifetime of shame ahead of him, so what he really wants to say is how much he loves him.

"Dad?" Alex yells.

Don can't seem answer. It's all he can do to stumble back and forth to keep his balance. The pain hasn't hit him. Maybe it never will, agony racing against adrenalin, shock, and death, but he takes a couple of steps in one direction then over compensates and stumbles back.

"Dad, I bagged a bear."

The whole thing reminds him of the day his mother tried to teach him to waltz. He had been hopeless and too young, but he'd wanted to learn, so she'd soldiered on, the two of them crashing around the living room, knocking over a lamp, stepping on each other's feet, spinning into the wall until they were laughing and laughing. They crashed onto the floor in a heap, Don stretched out across his mother's legs as if they were posing for a pieta.

Right now, Don has forgotten his mother's drinking and the dissatisfaction that seemed to be the driving force of her being. He has forgotten that she stopped talking to him for a year because he married Alex's mother. He has forgotten that in her last day of life, she seemed to have a single moment of clarity when she caught his eye and said, "I've never loved you."

What he remembers is that after their waltz, she said, "Well Donny, you might never be a dancer, but I promise you that you have a lifetime of joy ahead of you, a boy like you, so bright and beautiful." It makes him cry a little to think of it.

Alex crests the little hillock, and Don sees the recognition of what he's done move across his face. He knows that this is his chance to speak truth to his son.

Alex drops his rifle in the dirt and runs toward Don. He's going to fall, so he stumbles his last few steps in Alex's direction, who reaches out to catch him, this moment and the waltz merging somehow, becoming one thing. He can see the terror in Alex's face, feel it in the hands on his back the way a dancer can read love in the grip of his partner. This is the turning point of his son's life. These last words, Don thinks, will determine everything the boy does for the rest of always.

So Don opens his mouth. So Don speaks his words.

Second Place—*Broken Shackles at Her Feet*
Dean Gessie—Midland, Ontario

Adele's little devils demanded replica foam crowns for their Statue of Liberty visit. Nadine lost hers to the wind while waiting for the ferry. Her mother watched the crown cartwheel like a constellation through Battery Park, but there was nothing to be done. "I can't leave you two alone," she said, "and if we run after it, we'll lose our place in line!" Nadine said she didn't want to see the *stupid statue* without her replica foam crown, but Adele refused to separate interest from investment. "We must go! We have crown tickets!"

While boarding the ferry, Michael insisted on spinning his replica foam crown on his wrist. It was a boastful display meant to rub salt in his sister's wound. Unfortunately, he misjudged torque, friction and speed on a curved path. The replica foam crown leapt from its axis and cartwheeled like a constellation into New York Harbor. Michael wailed like a feral cat and, like his sister, became an anchor on his mother's arm. Adele elevated and yanked each forward, the gravity of despair no match for the weightless joy of crown tickets.

Even so, news of the apocalypse was a developing story. The children could not see Lady Liberty from their location on the ferry. Michael confirmed this fact while oxygenating bubbles from his nose, "I can't see the statue! You *promised*!" Nadine stopped crying long enough to say that everything was *rotten* and could they buy more replica foam crowns? Adele had no answer for the hubris of her children except a form of correction that improved the quality of their suffering: she read audibly and extensively from the Harbor Visitor Guide. Michael and Nadine howled and melted into puddles of grief on the ferry floor.

The children were first to notice the curious stranger. "What *stinks*?!" screamed one. "Oh, *polluted*!" screamed the other. The old man wore a replica foam crown vertically, stretched under his chin and around his skull. He looked like a wizened sunflower, both dead and alive.

Nevertheless, Michael and Nadine wondered privately if he would give *them* his replica foam crown because they were children and he was an old goat with a foot in the grave. For this reason, they held their noses and invited his approach. The stranger kneeled and hissed cruel and obvious testimony, "I have a crown and you don't."

And then Adele's ears roared with engine hum, bow splash and threshing wake. And the stranger's wizened sunflower face became a whirling pit of pitch and his replica foam crown a corona of fire. The children scampered to their mother's side, each looking mortified, blanched and obedient. Thereafter, all that remained of the stranger was a trail of mucus and brine and fingerprints that climbed the furthermost ferry rail. Adele embraced her brood as a hen her chicks and returned to the description of Lady Liberty in her Harbor Visitor Guide, that part that read, *broken shackles at her feet*.

Third Place — *The Wandering Wind*
Alan Berry — Harrison, Arizona

"What's going on?" Sonny rubs the sleep from his eyes. Momma stands above him. Light sneaks down the hall from the kitchen, backlights her blond hair, forms a halo around her round face. Her hand still holds his shoulder, "Put your shoes on. I've got your coat."

Sonny finds Momma at the front door. Her coat is buttoned to her neck, holding his. She helps him slip on his coat as the hall clock chimes once.

Momma closes the front door behind them. Sonny shivers as wind pushes up the legs of his pajamas. Momma opens the car door. He climbs in past the steering wheel. The car cranks over slow, starts. Sonny lays over in the seat, drifts back to sleep as the car warms.

Momma shakes Sonny. He fights to wake up. "Go in there and find your father." He follows her finger. A neon sign flashes "Entrance."

Under the flickering neon Sonny leans back, pulls with his full weight against the door. It opens enough for his small frame to dodge in. Cigarette smoke assaults him. Overhead lights reflect in hardwood lanes. Bowling pens hide in shadow. A man moves shoes from a counter to pigeon holes behind him. He notices the boy. "We're closed kid," a cigarette bounces in his lips. Sonny returns to Momma idling at the curb. She puts the car in gear. Sonny lays over in the seat. Sleep tugs at him. They hunt down another joint. Sonny pulls at a locked door. He looks to Momma. A toot of the horn says, "Come back to the car." They drive into the night.

A parking lot scattered with cars and a flashing "Cold Beer" sign offers promise to Momma. "Check one more time. Then we'll go home."

Sonny struggles through the door. Racks of bowling balls line a shadowy corridor. Yellow light, smoke and, *"A restless wind that yearns to wander, And I was born the next of kin,"* spill from a door at the far end.

Sonny stands in the yellow glare, sees Father hunched over a pin ball machine, working its buttons. A stranger with a brown bottle watches from the side. The ball escapes between the paddles. The machine's flashing lights and dinging vanish with it. Father digs in his pocket, gives the now smiling stranger a wad of bills. A painted woman appears beside Father, hands him one of the brown bottles she holds. Father turns into her, snuggles his face into her neck just as he eyes Sonny. Father's face drains. He makes space with the woman. She turns a stare to Sonny.

Father asks, "What are you doing here?"

Sonny struggles out, "Momma wants you to come home."

Father regains his swagger, "Tell her to go to Hell."

The woman makes more space with Father, "This your kid?"

Sonny doesn't hear the answer. Head down, he runs to clean air. Momma opens her door. As Sonny climbs over her, says, "He's not coming home."

Children's Chapter Books
Final Judge—Kay Whitehouse
DeLand, Florida

First Place—*Circus of Wings*
Elizabeth Buttimer—Atlanta, Georgia

Everyone asked Andy the same question.

His mother asked it.

His father asked it.

His grandparents asked it.

Often, friends of his family asked it.

Even people he just met wanted to know.

Everyone asked Andy the same question.

"What do you want to be when you grow up?"

When he said, "I don't know", they prompted him with more questions.

"Do you want to be a bus driver, a firefighter, a police officer?"

Maybe you want to be "a doctor? Or a teacher or a scientist?"

"Perhaps you would like to be a librarian or an accountant?"

"Or maybe you want to be something more exciting, like a comedian, a spy or a pilot?"

Questions, questions, questions, Andy was tired of questions.

He thought and thought and thought, again.

If everyone asked the same question, it must be important.

So, now he asked himself the question, "What do I want to be when I grow up?"

"I want to be something special, something unique." he declared.

Remembering the circus, he decided, I want to be an animal trainer but what animals do I want to train?

Tigers, that's it! I'll train tigers.

Then, he thought of their teeth. Too sharp. They might eat me.

No, not tigers.

Elephants, that's it! I'll train elephants.

Then, he thought of their size. Too big. They might sit on me.

No, not elephants.

Bears, that's it! I'll train bears.

Then, he thought of their claws. Too long. They might hug me too tightly.

No, not bears.

Lions, that's it! I'll train lions.

Then, he thought of their mouths. Too large. They might roar, loudly in my face.

No, not lions.

Horses, that's it! I'll train horses.

Then, he thought of their hooves. Too hard. They might step on me.

No, not horses.

What about camels? I'll train camels, that's it!

Then, he thought of their smell. Whew, they stink, and almost as bad, they spit.

No, not camels.

Perhaps something smaller.

Cats, that's it! I'll train cats.

Then, he thought of their independence. No one can herd cats.

They're too unruly.

No, not cats.

Dogs, that's it! I'll train dogs.

They're very obedient, man's best friend.

No, many people have dogs, too ordinary.

No one would come see us. They prefer their own dogs.

Andy paused to think and as he did, a butterfly landed on his arm.

Butterflies, that's it. I'll train butterflies.

I will be the best butterfly trainer in the world.

People will come from everywhere to see the show.

Holding up the butterfly, he called to the air

"Attention butterflies, come one come all,

I'm starting a circus and need your help.

Butterflies came from every direction and soon he had more than enough to train

He treated the butterflies well and they did their best

They loved to drink nectar from flowers so he grew plants and flowers that they liked.

2019 Seven Hills Review

First, they learned to fly together making patterns in the sky.

They fluttered into circles, hearts, flowers, and stars.

Then, they learned to fly like they do in air shows but slower and with more color.

They made big formations in the sky.

They even flew by color, first the reds, then the blues, then the yellows, oranges and browns.

Next, he made little perches for them from old spools of thread.

They sat on their perches and flapped their wings to music he played on a kazoo.

Flap first row

Flap, flap second row

Flap, flap flap third row

The fourth row danced on cue

He was the maestro and directed each butterfly group

"Perfect!" he would say and clap his hands.

The butterflies were very happy.

Andy also worked with them for the grand finale of the show.

It was a huge secret, a real crowd pleaser.

This finale was to make this, the best show in the world.

The day of the show came.

All the people who had asked him "What do you want to be when you grow up?" were invited.

Andy's family, friends, teachers and neighbors came.

The audience, eager to hear what Andy had decided to become, waited for his announcement.

Ladies and gentlemen, today I'll answer what you've wanted and waited to know.

I not only know what I want to be but I already do it now — I am a . . . I am a . . .

I am a . . .

Andy began to feel a funny rumbling in his tummy, his stomach felt like it was fluttering.

"One moment please," he turned his back to the audience and said to himself,

"I have one more set of butterflies to train."

He told his tummy to calm down and the butterflies in his stomach to relax.

"We have a show to do and I can't be nervous.

Calm down, the show must go on."

The butterflies in his stomach quit their flutter.

He turned to his audience and announced, "I am a butterfly trainer,

The Butterfly Maestro, the best butterfly trainer in the whole world.

And these are the world's best butterflies, The Circus of Wings."

"You are about to see the greatest show ever."

The butterflies gave their best performance

They flew by colors, they made shapes,

They did wing flapping and dance.

The audience was amazed by the circus.

Ready for the finale, they flew into straight lines above Andy

They hovered one atop the other and when Andy bowed,

They flared out into a peacock tail fan just over Andy's head.

Two butterflies flew with a banner for Andy that said,

"The Butterfly Maestro for The World's Best Butterflies."

This was the perfect finale for the Circus of Wings.

The audience clapped and clapped.

They all agreed, they had the answer to their question, even if Andy hasn't grown up yet.

He is "The Butterfly Maestro," the best butterfly trainer in the whole world.

Second Place—*The Treasure Hunt*
Christine Venzon—Peoria, Illinois

Oscar and his sister Gabrielle hurried along the sidewalk, breathless with excitement. "We're getting closer," Oscar said. Suddenly he stopped. He looked again at the screen of the electronic gadget in his hand. "This is the place!"

Gabrielle scanned the neat rows of leafy, green, growing things in front of them. "But this is Mr. Saheed's vegetable garden!"

Mr. Saheed appeared now, bursting between two tall sunflower plants. He wore canvas gloves and wide, straw hat. "Gabrielle! Oscar! What brings you here today?"

"We're geo-caching," Oscar said.

"Gee-oh-cashing?" Mr. Saheed repeated. "What's that?"

Oscar explained. "It's like a treasure hunt. Someone hides something and gives the longitude and latitude of the hiding place on a special website. Then we enter that information on this." He held up the gadget. "It's a GPS receiver. That stands for Global Positioning System. It uses satellites in the sky to make a map that shows the hiding place. The map led us here."

Mr. Saheed gazed at the large plot filled with vegetables. "You're welcome to look. But how will you know if you've found it?"

"The container is marked with a symbol." Gabrielle showed him the picture in their guidebook. "Four small squares, arranged to make a bigger square."

"And what do you do once you find it?"

"You write a note in the log book," she said. "Then you put it back for someone else to find."

Mr. Saheed looked alarmed. "You mean more people will be traipsing through my garden?" He winked slyly. "I'd better make lemonade."

Gabrielle and Oscar started the search. They parted the velvety soft leaves of tomato plants and the branches that were heavy with the round, red fruit. They lifted vines where skinny snap beans hung and inspected a row of bristle-headed broccoli. They handled all the plants with care – they wanted to enjoy the many tasty vegetables Mr. Saheed let them pick and take home all summer!

Finally, they sat to rest in the shade of some lima bean plants that twisted around wooden poles and towered over their heads. The breeze felt good on their skin. The air smelled sweet and earthy with growing things. They laughed at blackbirds in a birdbath, splashing the water and shaking themselves so their feathers stood out stiff and spiky. They watched bees creep into the orange, trumpet-shaped blossoms of squash plants.

Then Gabrielle saw something that made her frown. She pointed to a small, bell-shaped squash. "Is that a pineapple growing on a squash plant?"

"Pineapples don't grow – " Oscar began. But there it was: a bumpy, orange-brown pineapple lying among the yellow-gold squash.

He picked it up. "It's plastic," he said. His eyes popped. He showed Gabrielle: on the pineapple were four squares, arranged in a bigger square. "This is it!"

On the bottom of the pineapple was a large rubber plug. Oscar opened it and reached inside and pulled out a plastic bag with a small roll of paper.

"It's a scroll," Gabrielle said. She carefully unrolled it. "It says, 'Take time to smell the roses.'"

Oscar looked around. "Does Mr. Saheed grow roses too?"

"That's a saying," Gabrielle explained. "It means take time to enjoy things. Don't be in such a hurry."

"Having any luck?" Mr. Saheed returned, carrying a tray with three glasses of lemonade. He set the tray on a picnic table. Oscar and Gabrielle jumped up, eager to share their discovery.

"Mr. Saheed!" Oscar showed him the scroll. "Do you know about this?"

Mr. Saheed smiled and handed them their lemonade. "Yes, Oscar. I started this geocache."

"Why?" Gabrielle asked.

"I see so many people all wrapped up in their smart phones, playing video games or sending messages." Mr. Saheed wriggled his fingers like someone texting. "Sometimes they walk right into light poles! I wanted people to experience the world around them. See! Smell! Touch! And in my garden, there is plenty to see and smell and touch."

"And it's fun," Oscar added. "It felt like a treasure hunt too."

"And you pretended not to know about geocaching," Gabrielle said. "You had this planned all the time."

"That's clever," Oscar said. "Using a kind of video game to get people to stop playing video games."

"Not stop," Mr. Saheed said. "Just make time for other things too."

Gabrielle pulled a small notebook and pencil from inside the pineapple. "What should we write in the log book?" she asked Oscar.

"How about, 'And take time to taste the tomatoes and peppers.'"

"Quickly." Mr. Saheed nodded to a family with a GPS receiver walking towards them. "I think we're about to have company."

Gabrielle scribbled their note and returned the pineapple to the squash plant, as Mr. Saheed called to the newcomers. "Good morning! Beautiful day, isn't it?"

Third Place—*The Case of the Curious Tree*
Eneida Alcalde—Lebanon, Pennsylvania

In a purple world, full of purple things lived the Kuki Kakis. They bounced and danced, played and laughed under the purple sun shining over them. At night, the purple moon rose as the Kuki Kakis went to sleep. They dreamt purple dreams in their purple beds and woke to eat breakfasts of purple eggs and purple toast.

In this purple world, Kiki the Kuki Kaki walked to the Purple Forest every morning.

On one such morning, Kiki ran, skipped, and spun as she made her way deep into the woods to her favorite spot by a purple pond. Kiki sat near the pond. She looked around at the purple trees and the purple birds that flew high above in the purple sky. As she watched the birds flying in and out of the treetops, Kiki spotted a curious sight in the distance. It was a tree unlike any other she had ever seen. It was not purple.

Kiki ran to the curious tree and smiled when she reached it. The tree's many branches were full of not-purple leaves and its tall trunk was covered in not-purple bark. As Kiki wondered how the tree had appeared in the Purple Forest, a leaf fell from its branches and landed by her feet. Kiki picked up the leaf. It felt like any other leaf in her hands. But, as she traced its edges with her finger, her hands turned into the same color as the tree.

Soon her entire body turned into the curious color.

Kiki rubbed her arms, attempting to rub off the not-purple color, but it did not work. She ran back to the pond and dipped her hands into the cool water, but the not-purple color did not wash off. Instead, the pond turned into the not-purple color.

Kiki ran home to alert the other Kuki Kakis of this curious occurrence.

Once she reached the town, she spotted a pair of Kuki Kakis and approached them. They scowled and pointed at her:

"Who is that?"

"What is wrong with her?"

"Why does she look so different?"

Kiki ignored their questions and continued on, looking for help. The pair of Kuki Kakis followed behind her. As Kiki passed more streets, more Kuki Kakis scowled and pointed—and followed. In fact, by the time she reached her home, all the residents of the town gathered around her purple house. Kiki heard the Kuki Kakis whispering behind her back as she walked to the purple door of her house. She touched the purple doorknob. The entire house turned into the same color as Kiki and the curious tree.

The Kuki Kakis gasped: "Impossible!"

Kiki spun around to face the crowd.

The Kuki Kakis scowled and pointed at her: "How dare you come into our purple world!"

Kiki sighed: "But I am a Kuki Kaki! I went to the Purple Forest and found a not-purple tree. I touched one of its leaves and now I am the same not-purple color."

The Kuki Kakis screamed: "But everything is purple!"

Kiki pointed to her house: "My house is not purple." Kiki pointed to herself: "I am not purple."

The Kuki Kakis shouted: "Unbelievable!"

Kiki smiled: "I can prove it. Follow me!"

Kiki ran to the Purple Forest. The Kuki Kakis followed her through the town and into the woods.

When they reached the not-purple pond, Kiki looked around and spotted the curious tree. She pointed to it: "There!"

The Kuki Kakis shouted:

"We must get rid of it!"

"Chop it down!"

"Burn it!"

The Kuki Kakis ran to the tree. Kiki ran ahead of them. She stood in front of the tree and held out her not-purple hands, palms out. Kiki yelled: "STOP!"

The Kuki Kakis stopped their advance:

"But the tree is not purple!"

"We are a purple world!"

"Full of purple things!"

Kiki shook her head: "It doesn't matter. Every life is precious." She reached out her hand and touched the nearest Kuki Kaki. He turned into the same curious not-purple color.

He laughed and then touched the Kuki Kaki nearest to him. She also turned into the curious color. One after the other, the Kuki Kakis turned into the curious color.

In a matter of minutes, the entire purple land of the Kuki Kakis was no longer purple.

After much debate, the Kuki Kakis named this curious color: pink.

In this pink world, full of pink things the Kuki Kakis now live. They bounce and dance, play and laugh under the pink sun shining over them. At night, the pink moon rises as the Kuki Kakis go to sleep. They dream pink dreams in their pink beds and wake to eat breakfasts of pink eggs and pink toast.

Poetry

Final Judge – Josephine Yu
Tallahassee, Florida

First Place—Montecito Mudslide Toll Rises to 21

Isabelle Walker—Santa Barbara, California

Dear Mahogany forest,
in the drizzled nurture of Hawaiian Gods
you grow straight up to blue,
grass loafs at your feet
and drinks sun.

What do you know
of the lithified mountain,
squeezed of everything
buoyant and hopeful
until it forgets
the soft imprint of the girl's feet
on its spine,
the warmth of the boy's hand
as he hoists himself up,
the wary pimpled toad
in crevices,
oaks that had hung on
through dry years.
How could you understand
the heave of the mountain
casting all off
down a manhole to hell?

Dear Mahogany forest,
tell me,
in your slow procession to sky,
that crystal blue you are forever seeking,
is that where solace lies?

Second Place—Tempest

Hannah Yoest—Washington, District of Columbia

Her eyes are defined by rings—
they remind me of Liberty, because they are
the color of oxidized copper
holding a flame.

Sometimes they're like heat-
lightening. Far off systems in purple
clouds refusing to be engulfed by the night—
sporadic silky bursts pulsing through the static,

clinging to the air. Then thunder—
a stadium jumping to its feet.
Bleachers creak with the shift, as cheers
rise like worship.

Third Place—To the Angel Gabriel

Robert Brown—Decatur, Georgia

I've stopped asking,
I'll leave you alone.
Your work is done.
You took care of her
all those years –
I know you're tired.
Your wings are drooping
Your head hangs,
looking at the table,
last call, long drive,
one more Pall Mall
before you go.
Strike the match
on your eye teeth.
A shot of bourbon,
out into the night,
meeting at the Cathedral
with the other angels,
St. Michael, St. Peter,
St. John, St. James.

"A cat has nine lives," you told me,
"she's used them up."
You were in the room,
that last night, early morning,
"Now I lay me down to sleep . . ."
you mumbled to her.
And she was finished,
her body was finished,
yet her breathing continued
in the darkness.

We watched her, you and me.
Vita made it past her birthday,
twenty-nine,
her quiet breaths,
the train going by,
the star dust falling
and then she was gone,
she was silent,
she was still.

Haiku

Final Judge—Katya Taylor
Tallahassee, Florida

First Place—Giving Thanks
Jason Allen-Rouman—Palm Springs, California

Wedding china set

Plate, cup, saucer, bowl for twelve

Pass the memories

Second Place—Flood

Sara Zeller—Kenmore, Washington

lost in the roaring

water in a roadside ditch

one brown Teddy-Bear

Third Place — A Man on High Stilts

John Laue — La Selva Beach, California

A man on high stilts

Stares over the Fourth parade,

Takes a giant step.

Winning Authors

Eneida Alcalde – Lebanon, Pennsylvania

Eneide writes either long stories (over 6000 words) or very short ones (under 1000 words). "The Case of the Curious Tree" is one of her shorter pieces for children designed to be a picture book. Inspired by her Chilean-Puerto Rican background, she writes about people, animals, and magic. She's been a non-profit executive in Washington, DC and a returned Peace Corps Volunteer in Bolivia. She is currently a student in Harvard University's Extension School pursuing a Master's in Literature and Creative Writing. Her stories and poems have appeared in outlets such as The Potomac Journal, Stoneboat Literary Journal, and The Acentos Review.

Jason Allen-Rouman - Palm Springs, California

He writes:

I don't like titles
Haiku is simpler without
happy to conform

[apropos]

Rachel Bean – Tinley Park, Illinois

Rachel Bean is the the Content Editor for Cappex.com, a college a search site. She has her MA in Writing and Publishing from DePaul, as well as an MFA in Creative Writing from Fairfield University. She served as Editor in Chief for the Rockford University Regent Reporter and as a co-Editor in Chief for Fairfield U's literary magazine, CausewayLit. A proud Chicago suburbanite, Rachel lives with two rescued pups and spends her spare time working on YA literature. She also writes for Coffeeorbust.com, where she expresses her never-ending deep love for coffee.

Allen Berry – Harrison, Arkansas

Alan Berry is a retired industrial supervisor who found out that in the state of Arkansas, where he resides, college is free to residents aged sixty or older. One of the first courses he took was Creative Writing. His professor thought he had a unique writing voice and encouraged him in the classroom setting and beyond. With his professor's, and now friend's, mentoring, he continues to try to improve his writing skills.

Besides his new hobby of writing, Alan enjoys his thirty-year old Jeep Wrangler, teaching Taekwondo, fishing, and doing woodworking. With his wife Laura, a life long educator and encourager of his writing, Alan also enjoys their daughter, three dogs and one cat, bicycling, sailing, hiking, backpacking, and traveling.

John Brantigan – Walnut, California

John has spent the last five summers living off grid in a tent in the High Sierra, teaching poetry and writing for Sequoia and Kings Canyon National Park. This work comes out of the silence of that experience.

He is the first poet laureate of Sequoia and Kings Canyon National Park, and his work has been featured in hundreds of magazines and in Writer's Almanac and The Best Small Fictions 2016. I have eight books of poetry and fiction including *The Green of Sunset* from Moon Tide Press, and I teach at Mt. San Antonio College.

Robert Brown – Decatur, Georgia

A lifelong poet, Robert Brown has worked as a high school English teacher, a political organizer, driven a New York City cab, run the family business, sold balloons and a dozen other jobs that have worked their way into his poems. He has also written extensively about his life with his daughter Vita. He has read his work at the Folger Library in Washington, in Atlanta and in New York City.

DJ Buchanon – Tallahassee, Florida

At an age when most people are starting to think about retirement, DJ and her husband adopted Karalyn, an eight-year-old girl from Florida's foster care system. The experience of raising Karalyn and helping her heal from a very troubled past was the most intense and fulfilling period of her life. She started jotting down notes, and eventually used them to flesh out the interesting episodes, that built her book, *The Coming of Karalyn*.

Elizabeth Buttimer – Atlanta, Georgia

Elizabeth's poetry has been published in Magnolia Quarterly, Blue Mountain Review, Reach of Song Anthology, with pending publications in Pure Slush, Stoneboat and another Reach of Song. She received the Natasha Trethewey Award from the Atlanta Writer's Club.

Ashley Daugherty – Tallahassee, Florida

With tongue in cheek, and channeling MockingJay, she writes: Hello Sir and Madam, the guidelines say a cover letter or synopsis is not required yet I cannot submit without one. I do not wish to be disqualified so good luck to all and "May the odds be ever in your favor."

Rebekah Davis – Bishop, California

Rebekah has one published autobiographical memoir entitled *Becoming Kimberly, a Transgenders Journey.* She works professionally as a Nuclear Medicine Technologist and has setetled in Bishop after several stops as a traveling nurse. A widow with three grown sons, and several grandchildren, she have always wanted to write and began a couple of years ago to work on her first book. Life changes, including the death of a beloved spouse created both the background for the memoir and the time to write it.

With the publication of my first book behind me, I turned my attention to the next chapter in my literary career. The work in progress is titled "Collision Orbit"

Jacqueline Hope Derby

Jacqueline is a writer, minister, and former healthcare chaplain. A graduate of Duke Divinity School, her professional areas of interest include sudden traumatic loss, resilience and grief, liberation theology, the persistence of hope and creativity, and the spiritual musings of children. She's been published in *Whatever Works: Feminists of Faith Speak,* and she has been a national speaker on healthcare worker resilience. She and her family live in Kentucky.

Richard Fellinger – Camp Hill, Pennsylvania

Randy is an award-winning indie author, college writing instructor, and former journalist. His first novel, *Made to Break Your Heart*, was published last year by Open Books after being named a finalist for the Somerset Novel Award. His short story collection, *They Hover Over Us*, was published in 2012 after winning the Serena McDonald Kennedy Award. He's also a Pushcart Prize nominee, winner of the 2008 Flash Fiction Contest at Red Cedar Review, and teaches writing at Elizabethtown College.

Robert Fogler – Armed Forces, Pacific

Originally from Ohio, Robert Fogler currently lives in Cambodia with his husband and two spoiled dogs. While overseas, he is working on getting his MFA in Writing. You can see his antics on Instagram @eddiewritesthings.

Dean Gessie – Midland, Ontario

Dean has been a prize winner in multiple international contests. Dean's short stories have appeared in anthologies in Ireland, England and the United States. He has also published three novellas: *Guantanamo Redux* is dystopian fiction about the current political climate and near future in America; *A Brief History of Summer Employment* is a fictional memoir; and *TrumpeterVille* is animal allegory and political satire.

Brett Herrmann – Spring Valley, Illinois

Brett Herrmann was born and raised in the small town of Spring Valley, Ill. He attended Illinois Valley Community College and received a Bachelor's Degree in creative writing from the University of Illinois at Urbana-Champaign. He currently works as a reporter for the La Salle NewsTribune and, in the past, worked extensively in the fried chicken business.

Francis Hicks – San Antonio, Texas

Francis writes poetry and short fiction which give him great pleasure. His first novel "Pay Attention" is complete and his second is well underway. He is a member of The Writer's League of Texas and The San Antonio Writer's Guild. His prose has won awards and his poetry is included in "The Way The Light Slants" anthology.

Liz Jameson – Tallahassee, Florida

Liz Jameson spends most of her time editing – she is an editor for the Florida Department of Elder Affairs by day and a freelance editor by night. She is also writing a memoir based on the theme of resilience in the face of abandonment and loss. Additionally, she enjoys writing humorous essays for her blog. She was awarded the Josephine Mellichamp Memorial Award by the Council of Authors and Journalists, Inc., and has received other recognitions for her writing. She has been a member of the

Tallahassee Writers Association since 1996 and served as president and conference chair.

John Laue – La Selva Beach, California

John Laue, teacher/counselor, a former editor of Transfer and Associate Editor of San Francisco Review has won awards for his writing beginning with the Ina Coolbrith Poetry Prize at The University of California, Berkeley. With five published poetry books, a sixth coming out next year, and a book of prose advice for people diagnosed as mentally ill, he presently coordinates the reading series of The Monterey Bay Poetry Consortium, and edits the online magazine Monterey Poetry Review.

Michael Pesant – Ashville, North Carolina

A graduate of the University of North Carolina by the narrowest of margins, Michael Pesant lives, works, and writes in Asheville. His essays and short fiction have been published in The Acentos Review, Youth Imagination, Junto Magazine, and elsewhere.

Crew Scheilke – Bloomfield, New Jersey

A native of New Jersey, Crew Schielke is a second generation attorney and brown belt in Brazilian Jiu Jitsu. You can find him in his secret chamber early each morning spinning tales before he heads off to court to fight for his clients and acquire new material for his first calling.

Christine Venzon – Peoria, Illionois

Illinois native, Christine Venzon is a freelance writer and former textbook editor whose work has appeared in general interest and Christian magazines including *St. Anthony Messenger, Appleseeds,* and *Odyssey*. She was a contributor to the food encyclopedia, *Entertaining: From Ancient Rome to the Super*

Bowl. She has won awards for her children's fiction from *Highlights for Children* magazine, and was runner-up in the Saturday Evening Post Great American Fiction contest in 2014 and 2017. Her personal and professional interests include food history, food science, social and environmental justice, and Cajun and Creole culture, a passion she cultivated while living in Southwest Louisiana.

Isabelle Walker – Santa Barbara, California

Isabelle began writing poems ten years ago, after adivorced. Fortunately, she made the most of the upheaval by enrolling in a Master's of Fine Arts in Creative Writing program. In addition to poetry, Isabelle also writes essays, one of which, "*A Pine Branch*," was published in The Tishman Review last July. She earned that MFA in Creative Nonfiction and Poetry from Antioch University Los Angeles last summer.

Hannah Yoest – Washington, District of Columbia

Hannah is a writer and editor living in Washington D.C., where she works for a weekly magazine. She graduated from the University of Virginia where she studied fine art photography and political science. She also studied and workshopped poetry with Josh Bell at the Iowa Writers Workshop summer course.

Sara Zeller – Kenmore, Washington

Sara attended college at Washington State University, majoring in Humanities and English Literature. She spent much of her professional career teaching and tutoring at all levels, from college-level writing at Washington State to teaching Elementary Library and Pre-Kindergarten. In college, Sara lobbied in Washington D.C., worked as a Wildland Firefighter, and led re-planting and bio-engineering projects for Environmental Projects at Washington State.

Sara Zeller is a Writer, Editor, and stay at home Mom. Sara writes prose and poetry in a broad range of subjects and genres. Sara draws much of her creative writing inspiration from Artistic pursuits and Nature.

2018 Finalist Judges

When possible, we have been adding a feature to our annual publication, an interview with one of our judges. In 2016, we featured Florida's Poet Laureate. This year we are pleased to add some additional information on our long running judge for Flash Fiction, Anna Yeatts. Any writer can tell you that developing character, scene, and story are all important. Doing that in five hundred or so words takes a special talent. So, we've asked Anna a few questions about herself and the craft.

An Interview with Anna Yeatts – Flash Fiction

Anna is the publisher of *Flash Fiction Online*, an online magazine for both literary and genre stories. Her own short fiction runs the gamut from horror and dark fantasy to more experimental, literary pieces. Anna's background is in biology and anatomy — always helpful when writing and reviewing body horror. She blogs occasionally for SF Signal's *Mindmeld*, the FlashBlog, and anywhere her opinion is allowed. Though Anna forever hopes to channel Shirley Jackson from the ether into her laptop as she searches for that perfect story, she recognizes this is a quest that will take a lifetime and beyond. Anna hides out in Pinehurst, North Carolina.

7H: I have questions, but first, I'd like to know a little about Anna Yeatts and how she got into flash fiction. Something a little more elaborate than an official bio, but not a memoir. Ya know?

Anna: In 2011, I started at Flash Fiction Online after seeing a call on Codex asking for slush readers. I was pretty new as a writer and had heard that reading slush was a good way to get better at your own stories. I immediately fell in love with flash because it was so hard to do well, and yet when it was, it could be as impactful as much longer pieces. Jake Frievald left FFO in 2013 and I took over as Publisher. It's been a whirl-wind ever since.

7H: What do you see as essential in a flash fiction piece? Is it hook? Surprise?

Anna: For me, it's voice. With such a limited word count, you can't tell the reader everything they need to know in straight exposition. But a great voice will imply an entire world of backstory while still moving the plot forward.

7H: Any general thoughts about creating those existential works that have impressed you?

Anna: The best flash seems to be multi-layered. It's immersive, beautifully written, tells a complete story, and is thought-provoking.

7H: Thinking about *Bear Waltz*, you gave it Number 1. What struck you about that scene in the woods?

Anna: In *Bear Waltz*, I really liked the way the two plot lines mirrored one another within one narrative. It was very well structured and the author delivered enough of a resolution so the emotional payoff was there. The main character, Don's point of view was deep enough to let the reader feel Don's emotional reactions (and at times, physical pain) but it never went over that line into melodrama.

7H: Your Second Place choice, *Broken Shackles at Her Feet*, was a little hard to interpret, hard to figure what that last paragraph or two was about. Did you find something quirky in that? Did that imprecision leave you unsatisfied?

Anna: Maybe because *Flash Fiction Online* gets primarily genre fiction, I didn't have trouble believing that the man on the ferry was supernatural. I usually don't like mother/child stories because they lean too cutesy and the stakes aren't high. But this one did a good job of taking the reader's expectations—that the children were innocent and sweet—and turning it back on the reader in a rather startling way. I thought the ending worked well with what I assumed to be the mother's knowledge that yes, her children really are devils in their own way and that they were her shackles. But if she'd said all that outright, it wouldn't have been as interesting.

7H: *Wandering Wind* is especially poignant. The mother sends her kid into several dives looking for his dad, her husband. Seemed longer than it was. Your thoughts?

Anna: The voice in *Wandering Wind* is quite good. The setup is as well. For me, the point of view could have been deeper. I didn't know how Sonny felt as he looked for his dad. And I really wanted some emotional breadcrumbs from Sonny to tell me if I was supposed to be angry or sad or hopeful. When the point of view isn't deep enough, a story often doesn't feel "sticky" enough. That might be why it felt longer.

7H: You've been our judge for about five years now, what do you see happening in the genre? Is it morphing? I've seen requests for things in 60 words or less. That's not even a bad TV ad. What's with that?

Anna: I think social media is part of that trend. We're all trying to be pithy and entertaining in an Instagram caption or a Tweet. I've seen a lot of experimental formats playing with stories told through social media. Some have been more successful than others. It's hard to tell a story without the atmospheric details we're used to in our prose.

7H: Lastly, can we please have you as our judge of the 2019 contest, and is there an outlet beyond the Yahoo Crwropps listserve that you can recommend to get our promo out?

Anna: I'd love to come back again next year! And I've found the best way to get information out to the most writers possible is again… social media. At FFO, I get messages from other publications asking for a signal boost, and we try to do as much as we can.

7H: Yea!

Darryl Bollinger – Adult Novel Excerpt

Darryl Bollinger grew up in Macon, GA. He received an undergraduate degree in accounting and started work at a for-profit hospital company in 1975, his introduction to the health care industry.

While working full time, he earned a master's degree in Health Care Administration from Trinity University in 1986. Over his twenty-eight years in health care, he worked in a number of different management positions with a variety of health care companies, including vendors, consulting firms, and a large not-for-profit health care system. In 2010, he decided to embark on a writing career.

He is an award-winning author of six novels, all medical thrillers. Darryl and his wife live in the mountains of western North Carolina, where he is working on his next novel.

He is former president of Tallahassee Writers Association, a member of Florida Writers Association, Florida Authors and Publishers Association, and The Writers' Workshop of Asheville. www.darrylbollinger.com

Patricia Charpentier – Creative Non-Fiction

Owner of Writing Your Life and LifeStory Publishing, sister companies devoted to publishing personal and family history writing, Patricia offers ongoing workshops and classes, including programs that utilize videos, group and one-on-one coaching, and is a popular speaker and seminar leader throughout Florida and South Louisiana. She's published three other booklets related to life story writing, and her work has been anthologized numerous times. Her byline has also appeared in a variety of periodicals.

Patricia holds an M.A. in creative writing from the University of Central Florida and a B.A. in journalism from Louisiana State University and has worked as a memoirist, writing coach, editor, writing instructor, journalist and photographer. She also had a twenty-eight-year career in mortgage banking information technology. Originally from South Louisiana, Patricia now lives in Orlando, Florida with her husband Bob. She loves to dance for exercise but is grateful that the motto of the studio is: There are no mistakes, only solos. patricia@writingyourlife.org

Saundra Kelley – Short Story

A descendant of multiple generations of North Floridians, Saundra Kelley is a performer in the oral tradition of Spoken Word. She is the author of three books and in all of them her love of the natural world is a prominent focus. She took her undergraduate degree in the Social Sciences from Florida State University, and had a career in the non-profit sector. In 2006, she left Tallahassee to pursue a masters degree in Performance Art with a storytelling concentration at East Tennessee State University. After graduation, she stayed on for ten years , becoming a member of the Jonesborough Storytellers Guild Performance Troupe, and serving three years as its president. Since returning to Tallahassee in 2016, she has authored two books and has become very active in TWA, after a busy year as its president, is now 'relaxing' as our immediate past president.

S.R.Staley – Young Adult Novel Excerpt

Sam Staley is the author of 13 nonfiction and fiction books, including the young adult action/adventure series the Pirate of Panther Bay. His books have earned more than 10 literary awards. He has served on the faculty of the Florida Writers Association and conducts workshops on what writers can learn about storytelling from film, the use of foreign language do differentiate characters, and balancing action with description to provide forward momentum in story-telling. In addition to his pirate series, his current projects include forthcoming nonfiction book book on The Beatles. He is active on Facebook (SR Staley), Twitter (@SamRStaley), Instagram (@samuelrstaley), and www.samuelrstaley.com.

Katya Taylor – Haiku

Katya Sabaroff Taylor, M.Ed., is a writer (especially fond of haiku, but also short stories, essays, and other poetry forms), who has been offering creative writing (LifeStories and Haiku poetry) around Tallahassee since 1990. She is the author of Journal Adventure Guidebook, My Haiku Life and Prison Wisdom, a compilation of writing done behind bars with inmates. She believes we all have a writer within us, and she enjoys the creative alchemy that happens when people write together. Please visit her website at creativeartsandhealing.com for more details.

Joesphine Yu – Poetry

Josephine Yu earned an MFA from Georgia State University and a PhD from Florida State University. Her first manuscript, *Prayer Book of the Anxious*, won the Judge's Prize of the 15th Annual Elixir Press Poetry Awards and will be published in 2016. Her poems have appeared in such journals as *Ploughshares*, *The Southern Review*, *TriQuarterly*, and *Best New Poets 2008*. She won the Ploughshares 2013 Emerging Writers Contest and has been honored with Meridian's 2010 Editor's Prize, the New Letters 2010 Poetry Award, and the New Letters 2010–2011 Readers Award for Poetry.

Kay Whitehouse - Children's Chapter Book

Kay Whitehouse lives in DeLand, Florida with her standard poodle, Bear. She is involved in commercial real estate, has written a book on real estate, a romance novel and a children's multi award winning series called, "A Hand Truck Named Dolly." Writing and creating stories, as well as country music songs, is Kay's passion. She is an independent publisher and an active member of the Florida Authors and Publishers.

2018 Reading Committee

A huge thank you is owed to our first readers. All are members in good standing of the Tallahassee Writers Association and contributed, in some cases, considerable time in reviewing and pre-judging the submissions. These guys are the best!

Doug Alderson	Iain Baird
Melanie Barton	Alice Cappa
Faith Eidse	Robert Gibbs
Rhiannon Green	Nancy Hartney
Liz Jameson	Joshua Jordan
Richard Junior	Tom Pelham
Ghasi Phillips	Charles Veneble
Sydney Watson	Gale Workman
Pat Zick	

2019 Seven Hill Literary Contest
Penumbra Poetry & Haiku Contest

$\rightarrow$ Call for Submissioins! $\leftarrow$

Seven Hills Literary Contest

Novel Except: 3,000-word maximum, any genre; first chapter. Please add a 150-word (or less) plot synopsis at the beginning of the document.

Young Adult Novel Excerpt: 3,000-word maximum, any genre; first chapter. Please add a 150-word (or less) plot synopsis at the beginning of the document.

Creative Non-Fiction: 3,000-word maximum, sub-missions in this genre could include (but are not limited to) memoir, food or travel writing, personal essays, news journalism, biography, non-fiction stories, and nature writing. The emphasis in creative non-fiction is on factually true yet elegant literary expression.

Short Story: 3,000-word maximum. An economy of setting and precise narration.

Childrens's Picture Book: 2,500-word maximum. Please add a 150-word (or less) plot synopsis at the beginning of the document. (No pictures)

Flash Fiction: 500-word maximum.

Penumbra Poetry and Haiku Contest

Poetry: Up to 50 lines, any style or subject; line length may be edited to fit final publication format.

Haiku: 3-line haiku need not conform to strict syllable count.

Prizes: All literature and Poetry Prizes:
1st – $100, 2nd – $75, 3rd – $50
Haiku: 1st – $60, 2nd – $40, 3rd – $30

Seven Hills is a general circulation publication; NO X-rated materials will be accepted. It is a blind publication; any evidence of the author's identity in the primary submission will disqualify the submission. Please provide a 150- to 200-word biography with your application: emphasis on who, what, why; your inspirations and aspirations; a little horn-tooting acceptable.

Deadline for Submissions: August 31, 2019

All submissions must go through the Submittable website:

https://sevenhillsreview.submittable.com/submit

Notes